The Fullness of Truth

To the greater glory of God,
Who is Three in One,
Blessed forever

The Fullness of Truth

Catholicism and the World's Major Religions

REV. THOMAS M. KOCIK

NEWMAN HOUSE PRESS

FIRST EDITION
Published in 2013 by
Newman House Press
601 Buhler Court
Pine Beach, New Jersey 08741

ISBN 978-0-9881888-1-5

Printed in the United States of America

Contents

Preface

THE literature on world religions is immense, and numerous apologetic works defend "the faith which was once for all delivered to the saints" (Jude 3). This book combines those two themes, providing a Christian and specifically Catholic apologetics within the study of other religious traditions. It is thus neither a systematic presentation of Catholicism nor a disinterested examination of other religions and other forms of Christianity. Rather, it seeks wisdom wherever wisdom can be found, all the while pointing to the fullness of truth contained in the Christian revelation, by which all partial and hazy truths are found wanting. This truth, paradoxically, includes the recognition that it is impossible for us to exhaust the truth.

In the course of this work, I have tried to avoid the mistakes to which studies of comparative religion are prone: tearing down firm boundaries, imagining links on the basis of superficial similarities, interpreting all religious themes as metaphors and none as literally true, and confusing objectivity with neutrality. I have also taken care to represent fairly the enormous range of mythologies and revelations bunched together under the term "religion." Apologetic interest need not preclude sympathetic study. Nor should it rest on the illusion that all reasonable people will agree about their religious convictions once they have been shown the error of their ways. Disputes about religious beliefs cannot in every instance be dismissed as the result of sin, pride, or obstinacy. Christianity, so Christians believe, presents the world with a doctrine, a system of worship, a law, a grace, and a sanction that are not of this world, but of a supernatural character. While its teaching is aided by reason and surrounded by external evidence, historic and documentary, the intrinsic truth of its teaching baffles all attempt at human demonstration and appeals only to faith, which is a gift of God.

Let us take a rapid glance at the essential teaching of Christianity. According to it, the only true God, Creator and Lord of Heaven and earth is the Most Holy Trinity—almighty, all-knowing, uncreated, eternal, indivisible, and infinite Love subsisting in three eternally distinct and co-equal Persons: the Father, Son, and Holy Spirit. Christianity confesses no other God. And because one cannot respond in faith and love to a divine It, the chief object of Christ's mission to this world was the revelation of this unfathomable mystery of the one only God whose very essence is Love because He is a loving communion of Persons.

The ultimate revelation of God is Jesus Christ, the Second Person of the Divine Trinity, God the Son who assumed a human nature in the womb of the Blessed Virgin Mary. And this God-man submitted to the shame of the Cross and rose from the dead for the world's redemption from the clutches of sin, death, and Satan—mysteries of infinite love and power transcending human thought. Furthermore, the mission of the Holy Spirit to this world—the coming down of the Third Divine Person, sent by Christ to abide forever with the faithful, and who, from the day of Pentecost until the end of time, renders testimony to Christ's identity and Gospel in the Church's enduring triumph over the combined opposing forces of the world.

And its worship: the public worship instituted by Christ finds its source and apex in the Christian sacrifice, a worship without earthly peer—being as it is no less than the living, divinized humanity of Christ, substantially present in the Eucharist, and offered up to God by the hands of Christ's own divinely transmitted priesthood in perpetual commemoration and individual application of the Redemption accomplished on the Cross of Calvary.

And the Gospel: the law of Christ, the moral code of the Kingdom of God, a law which crucifies man's fallen nature in order to elevate souls to a height of virtue inaccessible to all human effort; a law whose fulfillment by countless thousands of every condition in every Christian age and place has created an army of saints and reproduced among them the moral beauty of Christ.

And the gift of grace: a supernatural force enabling the soul to fulfill the highest Christian duty and virtue; a gift conveyed through the sacraments, those supernatural institutions of Christ surely conferring on the recipient, who places no obstacle, a holiness that is nothing less than a partaking of the divine nature.

Finally, the virtue of faith: the divine faculty enabling the mind to affirm the truths revealed by God; a supernatural light infused into the soul at Baptism, manifesting with a divine certainty the truth of all Christian teaching; a certainty resting, not on the shifting sands of human opinion, but on the everlasting rock of God's own infinite knowledge and veracity.

This superhuman certainty of faith is sustained from without as experience and reflection deepen our knowledge of revealed truth and of the Church, whose unity of faith and claim to the infallibility of her divine Head reflects the unity and consistency of the mind of Christ. The Church's moral teachings and her innumerable saints reveal the evidence in Christianity of the indwelling spirit of Christ, indeed of the Holy Spirit. And her presence worldwide testifies to Christ's universal sovereignty; while her unbroken, historical continuity bears out Christ's promise to abide with His Bride forever and lead her into all truth.

The Trinity, the Incarnation of God's Son, the redeeming Sacrifice mystically renewed upon the Church's altars, the grace-bearing sacraments, the privileges of the Virgin Mother, the new life of the world to come—the intrinsic evidence of these unfathomable doctrines exists only in the infinite mind of God; hence when revealing them to the world the Son of God and Son of Mary commanded us to accept them on the authority of the Church which He founded upon the Apostles headed by Saint Peter. This is Christianity. And as I hope to have shown in an indirect way, this is Catholicism if it is anything.

In the course of my research, I visited no temple, mosque, or synagogue; nor did I interview Hindu gurus, Confucian sages, or Pentecostal preachers. I did, however, rely heavily on the works of scholars who devoted years to doing all those things, and I spent countless hours consulting official denominational publications and websites. Janet Florick's thoughtful advice on methodology was likewise helpful and greatly appreciated. I wish also to acknowledge the Reverend Fathers Roger J. Landry, executive editor of *The Anchor* (the newspaper of the Diocese of Fall River, Massachusetts), for inviting me to contribute the biweekly series from which this book originated, and Peter M. J. Stravinskas, Ph.D., S.T.D., founder of Newman House Press, for recognizing the merits of this study and bringing it together between two covers.

I

PRELIMINARIES

THERE are many possible answers to the question why one should become and remain Catholic. Among these are Catholicism's rich spiritual and liturgical life, its communal spirit, its optimistic view of creation, its respect for human life at all stages, its openness to all cultures and peoples, its loyalty to the past, its sacramental imagination, its marriage of faith and reason, and its knack for maintaining unity in diversity. All good answers, these—but none of them gets to the heart of the matter. When all is said, the most compelling reason for embracing Catholicism—or any religion, for that matter—is the belief that it is *true*. The flipside, logically, is the judgment that all other religions are false, or at least less true. As G. K. Chesterton's fictional Father Brown said, "I do believe some things, of course . . . and therefore, of course, I don't believe other things."[1]

Seeing the Whole in the Part

Either Jesus Christ is Lord of all or He is not Lord at all. What it means to say Jesus is Lord and live accordingly is something that has united and divided Christians from the start. Among the many brands of Christianity past and present, there is Catholicism. The word "catholic" means universal, as in pertaining to the whole. Catholic Christianity, as its name suggests, considers itself the fullest and truest expression of the faith which Jesus imparted to His first disciples and which, since apostolic times, has been believed, professed, and handed down from generation to generation of saints and sinners. Catholics see themselves as part of this living Tradition of Christian faith and life, a Tradition that encompasses, to varying degrees, the vast number of

---

[1] G. K. Chesterton, *The Incredulity of Father Brown* (Cornwall, Eng.: House of Stratus, 2001), p. 146.

Christians beyond the Catholic fold, principally the Orthodox and Protestants. From the Catholic perspective, however, the apostolic Tradition is incomplete without the ministry of Peter (the papacy) and some other distinctively Catholic things. To put it boldly, Catholicism embodies the fullness of divinely revealed truth.

Not the exclusive truth, but the *fullness* of truth—a crucial distinction. From Saints Justin Martyr through Athanasius and Augustine to Thomas Aquinas, the great Christian theologians understood that all truth is the truth of Christ, the eternal Word who enlightens everyone.[2] Whatever knowledge of God exists outside Christianity is, in the Latin phrase, *semina Verbi*, "seeds of the Word" liberally sown by the Spirit who blows where He wills.[3] These seeds come to full flowering in Christ, whose mystical body is the Church. Since there is only one Christ, there can be, at the deepest level, only one Church. In both the Apostles' Creed and the Nicene-Constantinopolitan Creed professed by Catholics, Orthodox, and many Protestants, the Church is described as "one, holy, catholic, and apostolic." Catholicism claims to be that Church—not just one among many branches or manifestations of Christ's Church, but the Church of the creeds in all its fullness. Does this mean that, in the Catholic view, all non-Catholic Christians are entirely outside the Church? Far from it. For just as Catholicism acknowledges elements of truth and grace among non-Christian peoples (the *semina Verbi*),[4] so it recognizes elements of the one Church—the Catholic Church—in other Christian communities.[5] It is not, then, a matter of "all or nothing" but of "all or less." Yes, there are many reasons for living and dying as a Catholic, but the best reason is believing that Catholicism is the "all" its name signifies.

"What knows he of England who only England knows?" asked the well-traveled poet Rudyard Kipling, suggesting that we know ourselves better when we know others. If that is true, then we Catholics stand to gain from learning about other reli-

[2] See John 1:9.

[3] See John 3:8.

[4] Second Vatican Council, Decree on the Church's Missionary Activity, *Ad Gentes*, no. 9.

[5] Second Vatican Council, Dogmatic Constitution on the Church, *Lumen Gentium*, no. 8, §2; Decree on Ecumenism, *Unitatis Redintegratio*, no. 3, §2.

gious traditions. That is the aim of this book. We will start by observing the intellectual climate prevalent in our Western culture, which takes Pilate's cynical question, "What is truth?" to be a discussion-stopper. After exploring the possibility of knowing truth, including religious truth, we will explore the major non-Christian religions, allowing the seeds of the Word reflected in them to point us to the truth (there's that word again) fully revealed in Christ. Then we will turn our attention to the major Christian traditions outside Catholic unity, discovering how the Gospel truths professed and lived in those communities turn out, in the end, to be at their strongest and richest within the full stream of Tradition that is Catholicism. By discovering something of our own in what is alien, I believe we can better understand ourselves in light of what we have received. The result, please God, will be a faith that is more vibrantly catholic—and Catholic.

Comparative Religion vs. Comparatively Religious

Monsignor Ronald Knox, a convert from Anglicanism and arguably the most brilliant English Catholic writer of the twentieth century, famously quipped that the comparative study of religions "is an admirable recipe for making people comparatively religious."[6] There are two ways to understand this. When, for example, we learn of similarities between Christianity and the pre-Christian myths that tell of gods who descend to earth, die, and are resurrected, we might be led to infer that the Christian religion is simply a recasting of old myths and nothing more, in which case we will have lost our faith. In fact, the resemblance of certain pagan myths to the Passion and Resurrection of Jesus was used as an argument against Christian faith from the earliest days of the Church. Those who discredit Christianity as mythical would have us believe that the stories of Dionysus, Attis, Adonis, Osiris, and Jesus are all variants of the same primordial theme.

Another way of understanding what Knox had in mind is to turn the table. Rather than read the Christian Gospel in the light

[6] Ronald A. Knox, *The Hidden Stream: Mysteries of the Christian Faith* (San Francisco: Ignatius Press, 2003), p. 108.

of the world's myths, we might interpret myth in the light of the Gospel. From this perspective, we discover bits and hints of the truth fully revealed in Jesus Christ. Just as God spoke directly to Abraham and the Hebrew prophets, so, we might say, He planted "seeds of the Word" in the minds of pagan mythmakers to prepare the world for the coming of His Son in the fullness of time. Such was the view of the Church Fathers and later Christian apologists, including C. S. Lewis and J. R. R. Tolkein, both fine mythmakers in their own right. Whatever intimations of higher truth are contained in ancient mythology became historical fact in Jesus Christ. Or, to put it in biblical terms, "the Word became flesh and dwelt among us."[7]

Our faith can be more vibrant when we open our eyes to God's mysterious dealings with all peoples and cultures; we can then appreciate more deeply the fullness of God's saving truth as this comes to us from Israel to the Apostles and from one generation to the next within the Church. However, before launching into the major world religions, it is worth pausing to take notice of the prevailing intellectual climate.

Among those on the commanding heights of culture (as the Marxists used to say), especially in the universities, it is widely assumed that that there is no single, unifying, uppercase Truth. There is "your" truth and "my" truth, what "works" for you and what "works" for me; but *the* truth is either nonexistent or unknowable. From this assumption, it follows that "enlightened" spirituality does not revolve around any one concept of God; nor does it require that we believe in any one creed, any one set of doctrines, any one recipe for salvation, or, for that matter, any One. To quote the bumper-sticker version of the same, "God is too big to fit into one religion." And so we have the reason why countless spiritual seekers drift through the religious marketplace, sampling and browsing but never committing lest they miss out on something good.

The dominant philosophical mood has little patience for the idea of a God who cares whether and how we conceive Him, worship Him, and order our lives in His service. This raises obvious difficulties for serious Christians, Jews, Muslims, and everyone

[7] John 1:14.

else who believes it is just as possible to get it wrong in religion as in algebra. It is taken for granted that no one religion or philosophy can grasp the whole of reality.[8] There is a certain truth in that assumption, and we cannot afford to ignore it when considering Catholicism's claim to the fullness of truth. Therefore, as a final preliminary to our tour of the major religious traditions, we will explore the possibility and limits of human knowledge about God and the world. Only then will we be able to grasp and express the Catholic claim in an intellectually responsible way.

Think Responsibly

Contemporary Western culture has little patience for the idea of truth, especially religious or moral truth. The dominant philosophical mood is partly a result of the Enlightenment, which held that science is the only window onto reality, and partly a reaction against the pretensions of Enlightenment rationalism. It is considered a mark of sophistication to ask, with Pontius Pilate, "What is truth?" No answer is expected, and none will be tolerated. We are all left to follow our own real or imagined star. But rather than take Pilate's query to be a discussion-stopper, we might take it as a discussion-starter, an invitation to appreciate what it means to believe in truth and to embrace Catholicism as the fullness of truth.

So, what is truth? According to the classical definition that comes down to us from Greek philosophy, truth is the concordance of mind with fact, the knowledge of things as they really are. For example, my belief that there is beer in the refrigerator is true if and only if there is beer in the refrigerator. This theory of truth, endorsed by Saint Thomas Aquinas and other medieval luminaries, is often criticized as naïve because it simply assumes the mind's ability to know. Modern philosophy, which is typically said to begin with René Descartes in the seventeenth century, demands that we first prove the possibility of knowledge before making any statement about what is real or true.

---

[8] For a challenge to this assumption, which employs, uniquely to my knowledge, the "matter–form" theory of Scholastic philosophy, see my essay "Everything in Particular: A Metaphysics of Religious Pluralism" in *Second Spring: International Journal of Faith & Culture* 11 (2009): 36–45.

Aquinas, while allowing the possibility of human error, would have had little patience with this prerequisite. He was convinced that it is in the act of knowing something that we recognize our ability to know; we need no further guarantee of our ability to grasp truth than our awareness of the fact that we do indeed grasp it. Since Aquinas's thought holds pride of place in Catholic intellectual life, so much so that he is called the Common Doctor of the Church, our consideration of the fullness of truth will be based on his understanding of knowledge: The mind can know reality, including something of the ultimate, uncaused Reality we call "God." Nevertheless, if we are to speak responsibly of truth and its fullness, some clarifications are necessary.

In claiming the fullness of truth, Catholicism does not purport to be a Grand Unified Theory of Everything. The Church is concerned primarily with the truths revealed by God and believed by faith; for example, the Trinity. Philosophical and scientific theories, while valuable, are not the Church's first business. There is, however, a certain overlapping and interaction as regards the content of the various spheres of knowledge. The natural sciences tell us about ourselves and about the universe insofar as our five senses can take us. By reflecting on the finite things known through experience, we can infer the existence of an infinite Being on which all finite things depend. That is about as far as reason alone can go. There are "higher" questions that the particular sciences could never answer, such as the meaning of life and the nature of God. Divine Revelation, the highest truth, gives us knowledge of the truly ultimate; this is why theology, the study of God, was dubbed the "Queen of the Sciences" before the Enlightenment decoupled faith and reason.

Furthermore, human knowledge, scientific or otherwise, is constantly expanding and revising itself in light of new experiences and reflections. Newtonian physics, for example, was thought to be the final truth about the universe until Einstein and others came along. Even the infallible truths of revelation remain open to ever-deeper penetration, as Blessed John Henry Newman explained in his classic *Essay on the Development of Christian Doctrine* (1845). The living Tradition of Christian belief and practice unfolds against the horizon of eternity. We see through a glass darkly in anticipation of our meeting Truth face to face.[9]

Strictly speaking, therefore, the fullness of truth can be none other than the contemplation of God in the Beatific Vision of Heaven. When affirming Catholicism as the fullness of truth, we must bear in mind the limits and fallibility of human knowledge, even if that knowledge turns on a revelation of divine information. But enough of preliminaries. We are poised to launch our exploration of the major religions, guided by faithful thinking and thinking faith.

[9] See 1 Corinthians 13:12.

II

EASTERN RELIGION

THE word "religion" derives from the Latin *re + ligare*, "to bind back," meaning to restore, by public and communal worship, a lost intimacy between worshipers and the Divine. This was the ordinary understanding of religion in the pre-Christian Mediterranean world. Among the Latin-speaking Christians in late antiquity who adopted this view, religion meant "things like Christianity." Judaism was of interest primarily as a precursor to the Good News, and Islam, which came into existence in the seventh century, was deemed more a Christian heresy than a new religion.[10] A millennium would pass before European explorers and missionaries would effectively make known to their countrymen the spiritual beliefs and practices of the Far East, Africa, and the Americas. The Chinese had exotic temples and highly developed ritual; the Indians prayed to countless gods and seemed to worship images of them; and so on. It seemed only natural to think of these patterns of belief as religions. Consequently, "religion" was treated as a genus of which there are many species, in the same way that dollars, pesos, and pounds are species of currency.

Truth be told, there is no widely shared understanding of what constitutes a religion or what it means to be religious. The usefulness of "religion" as a category is especially dubious when we study the belief systems of South and East Asia: Hinduism, Buddhism, Taoism, and Confucianism. Since in many ways these resemble philosophies or codes of ethical conduct more than religions, comparing them with Christianity is less like comparing apples to oranges than comparing fabrics to fish. Yet, even if our inherited idea of religion does not always seem to fit, we must have a frame of reference by which to compare and contrast.

[10] See, for example, John of Damascus, *Writings: The Fount of Knowledge*, trans. in *The Fathers of the Church*, vol. 37 (Washington, D.C.: Catholic University of America Press, 1958), pp. 153–160.

These Asian religions may not be religions in the sense we normally imagine, but neither are they science. Insofar as they have a vision of what constitutes paradise and instruct how to get there, our framework will do. More specifically, it is from the perspective of Catholic faith that we examine the bewildering panoply of religions, even as we try to see life through the eyes of those who adhere to other modes of belief.

Let us begin with the aforesaid religions of the East. While differences exist among them, they are unified in their view that ultimate reality is an impersonal, unknowable, all-pervading spirit. Only spirit is real; the material realm is an illusion grounded in ignorance. Individuality itself is illusory, because we are not really distinct from one another or from the Divine. Eastern religions do not profess a supernatural Being who created the world from nothing, guides creation, and commands obedience and homage. As the Hindu scholar D. S. Sarma explains, "The Supreme Being is a person only in relation to ourselves and our needs."[11] In other words, all attempts to personalize Divinity (the proverbial "three hundred thousand gods" of India, for instance) are feeble human projections onto the nameless and formless One.

And how do the Eastern religions view life's purpose? The ultimate goal of human life is to achieve mystical unity with the universal spirit. While this may be acquired through a variety of means, the one most familiar to Western peoples is meditation. Meditation is the practice of ridding the mind of any thought of the individual self as distinct from the universal spirit. Through a rigorous discipline, we can overcome the illusion of duality (distinct spiritual and physical realms) and thereby experience oneness with the One. This is termed "enlightenment."

Since "God" is impersonal, there is no real distinction between good and evil. Yet those who are wise recognize a practical code of conduct: by detaching themselves from the world of sense experience, they free themselves from enslavement to illusion and find enlightenment. Buddhist scripture states, "Those who love nothing and hate nothing, have no fetters."[12] Morality (if it

---

[11] D. S. Sarma, "The Nature and History of Hinduism," in Kenneth W. Morgan et al., *The Religion of the Hindus* (New York: Ronald Press, 1953), pp. 3–47, at p. 11.

[12] *Dhammapada*, chap. 16, trans. F. Max Müller, *The Sacred Books of the East*, vol. 10, part 1 (Oxford: Clarendon Press, 1881), p. 56.

can be called that) in Eastern religions is not about observing divine precepts, but attaining enlightenment so to fuse with the Absolute.

Perhaps nothing is stranger to us Westerners than the denial of the material realm. Easterners must find it equally strange that so many Western secular intellectuals, especially scientific materialists, deny the spiritual realm in declaring that all of reality is expressed in physics. Our chief concern, however, is theological. Starting with Hinduism, we will study the individual religions of the East, noting how their spiritual yearnings can point to the fullness of truth in Jesus Christ and His Church.

Hinduism

In the middle of the second millennium before Christ, Aryan tribes migrated to India from the north. The blending of their religion with those of the native Harappans and Dravidians (in northern and southern India, respectively) produced a potpourri of different gods and legends that would become the world's third largest religion after Christianity and Islam: Hinduism. Until the nineteenth century, the word "Hindu" had no specific religious meaning, and simply referred to the people living east of the Indus River, whatever their religious beliefs. It was only when the census introduced by the British colonial authorities in 1871 included Hindu as a religious designation that many Indians began to think of themselves as Hindu.

Hinduism has no single god whom all must worship, no fixed creed, no organized structure, and no single moral code. Yet Hinduism is not so internally diverse as to lack the basic contours that mark the religions of the East. It views divinity and the world as ultimately identical, and it considers the different world religions to be various attempts to get at the same thing. It is easy to see why Hinduism might appeal to spiritual seekers who crave religious experience but abhor orthodoxies.

Since it would be a feeble attempt to understand any religion or culture while ignoring its history, let us now examine the main stages of Hinduism's development. Hinduism underwent significant transformations during its long history, changing as it encountered new teachings, with minor gods evolving into major ones. The earliest period is the Vedic (from the Sanskrit word *Veda*, "knowledge"), roughly spanning 1500 to 500 B.C. This period is noted for the worship of many deities, some greater than others, though there is evidence of an earlier stage in which a creator god named *Dyaus-pitar*, the "Sky-father," was worshiped. (Note the phonetic resemblance to the Latin *Deus Pater*, "God the Father.") From the Vedic period come Hinduism's sacred texts, the Vedas. The earliest of these, the Rig Veda, is thought to be the world's oldest religious scripture and possibly the oldest document in any Indo-European language. It is a collection of hymns to the ancient gods, some of whom—Vishnu and Shiva, for example—became very important in later Hindu worship. Three other Vedas were composed featuring hymns, incantations, rituals, meditations, philosophical musings, and advice both spiritual and mundane. Attached to each of the Vedas are the Brahmanas, treatises instructing the priests how to carry out the sacrifices to the gods.

Toward the end of the Vedic period, a new set of writings was appended to the Vedas: the Upanishads. *Upanishad* means "those who sit near," and implies listening closely to the secret doctrines of a spiritual teacher. The Upanishads heralded a new stage in the history of Hindu religion. Whereas Vedic religion centered on the sacrifices to the gods, the Upanishads focus on philosophical questions such as the purpose of life and the nature of ultimate reality. They deny not only the reality of this world but also the reality of the individual self. The real self in me, in you, and in every apparently other person is not individual ego but *atman*, universal self, which is identical with *Brahman*, the "great one," the Universal Soul that permeates all things. To be one with Brahman is the goal of every human being. Unless we break free from all other desires, including the desire for existence as a distinct person, we are trapped in the illusion of individuality and so cannot unite with Brahman; we must instead be reborn into the world of appearances, either into a higher or lower caste, maybe even as an animal or plant. How we are reincarnated will be determined by *karma*, the cumulative effects of our good and bad deeds in one life.

Only with great effort could we escape from the cycle of birth-death-rebirth and enter the blissful state of *moksha*: the realization that nothing else but Brahman exists. This is to be obtained through *yoga*, a combination of mental and physical exercises whereby we tap our hidden divine energies and so come to pure awareness that our deepest self is not "I" but atman, which is Brahman: Atman is Brahman. This seems equivalent to saying that I am God. It bears repeating, however, that atman is not the individual self and Brahman is not the personal God of the Bible.

Classical and Later Hinduism

Having surveyed the earliest stages of Hinduism, let us now examine its subsequent history. The classical period,[13] roughly spanning 500 B.C. to A.D. 500, saw a trend toward the personification of the Divine. Brahman, the supporting ground of all life and being, becomes personal as Brahma, the creator of all. Vishnu represents the aspect of Brahman that preserves and sustains the universe. Shiva, the third god in the Hindu "trinity," is responsible for destruction and recreation.

Just as the Vedas and Upanishads were passed down orally for a long time before they were put into writing during the Vedic period, so the great legends of Hindu literature originated in oral traditions that were written near the end of the classical period. The Indian epic *Mahabharat*, which perhaps is the world's longest poem, and the *Ramayana* center around wars between human clans, as well as the conflicts of gods and demons: the entire cosmos, at every level, is involved in the struggle between order and chaos, good and evil. In the *Mahabharat*, Vishnu assumes both human and animal forms, one of which is his human incarnation as Krishna.

The best-known part of the *Mahabharat* is the *Bhagavad-Gita* ("Song of God"). Composed in the first century B.C., it remains the most popular source of religious inspiration for Hindus. Here, Krishna appears as the charioteer of the warrior Arjuna. He instructs Arjuna on his duty to fight in battle, on the nature of the soul, and on the ways to achieve *moksha*, release from the cycle of birth and rebirth. The best way is *bhakti*, loving devotion to a par-

---

[13] "Classical," "medieval" and "modern" are Western terms corresponding to Western divisions of history.

ticular god. *Jnana*, the way of knowledge or enlightenment, uses the techniques of yoga to gain a clear perception of one's deepest self (Atman) and God (Brahman). *Dhyana*, the way of meditation, concentrates on seeing through the illusion of differences. For those who find these paths too difficult there is *karma*—the way of works: doing one's duty unselfishly, without seeking personal gain.

During the medieval period, A.D. 500 to 1500, Hindu philosophy developed in different directions. The non-dualist school of thought, represented chiefly by Sankara (A.D. 788–820?), teaches that the real center of our being is not "I" but Atman, the transcendent Self, which is identical with Brahman.

A modified non-dualism was taught by the exceptionally long-lived Ramanuja (A.D. 1017–1137). As he saw it, Sankara's non-dualism makes *bhakti* impossible: if my deepest self is Brahman, logically, I should worship myself. This calls to mind Chesterton's quip: "That Jones shall worship the god within him turns out ultimately to mean that Jones shall worship Jones." [14] Ramanuja therefore held that the self is genuinely, if ambiguously, distinct from Brahman even after achieving *moksha*. At the same time, he described the self as a "distinguishing attribute" of Brahman.

The dualist school of Madhva (A.D. 1238–1317) goes even farther, asserting that Brahman, whom Madhva worshiped as Vishnu, is wholly other than the world. There is a real and abiding difference between God and the world, between God and the individual self, and between individual selves. Madhva's description of Vishnu's dealings with the human race will strike a chord with Christians: "The glorious Lord confers knowledge (on the devoted self) for his righteousness, and absolves him from sin and leads him to eternal bliss." [15] It should be noted, however, that dualism never entered mainstream Hinduism.

As a result of contacts with other cultures, Hinduism since medieval times has come to regard all religions as paths to the same truth (Christianity is an example of *bhakti*). Many modern Hindus will tell you that the different gods whose images they

---

[14] Gilbert K. Chesterton, *Orthodoxy* (New York: John Lane, 1908), p. 138.

[15] Madhva's commentary on the *Brahma Sutra*, in *A Sourcebook in Indian Philosophy*, ed. Sarvepalli Radhakrishnan and Charles A. Moore (1957; repr. Princeton University Press, 1989), p. 567.

venerate at home and in temples are but so many manifestations of the one God. The prayer of the priest opening temple ceremonies brings the relationship between Brahman and the various Hindu deities into focus: "You are without form, but I worship you in these forms." Moreover, the Indian saint Ramakrishna (A.D. 1836–86) perceived the same Savior figure in many different forms:

> The Saviour is the messenger of God. He is like the viceroy of a mighty monarch. As when there is some disturbance in a far-off province, the king sends his viceroy to quell it, so wherever there is a decline of religion in any part of the world, God sends his Saviour there.[16]

Accordingly, Hindus see Jesus as God's manifestation for the West and keep His image in many temples.

This historical synopsis has shown the bewildering variety within Hinduism. While any generalization is unsatisfactory, we can identify at least four marks of orthodox Hinduism. These are: (1) acceptance of the Vedas as containing eternal truth; (2) belief in reincarnation according to the law of karma; (3) salvation conceived as unity with Brahman; and (4) the variously valued paths of salvation: meditation with yoga exercises, selfless deeds, and devotion to any of Brahman's numerous manifestations.

Hinduism and the Gospel

Having gone through the major features of Hindu religion, let us use the light of Divine Revelation to search out the seeds of the Word present in Hinduism that point to the fullness of truth in Jesus Christ.

Hindus see the world as the result of a divine "play" that exists either merely as an appearance for the unenlightened mind or as the external body of Brahman. By contrast, biblical religion presupposes that we belong to a real world, distinct from our minds and from the Creator. Proverbs 8:30–31 suggests a certain playfulness of God's creative wisdom, but the universe also re-

---

[16] *The Sayings of Sri Ramakrishna*, compiled by Swami Abhedananda (New York: The Vedanta Society, 1903), as quoted, with minor editorial changes, in Huston Smith, *The World's Religions* (New York: HarperCollins, 1991), p. 74.

veals a love so great that, in George Weigel's fine phrase, "it burst the boundaries of God's inner life and poured itself forth in creation."[17] As for the world being God's body, a god who is of the same order of being as all else that exists is not the God of Genesis who spoke the universe into existence and now rules it by His providential care. Nonetheless, there is a seed of truth in Hinduism's awareness, vague though it is, that nature points beyond itself to a larger reality, namely, the God who is love.[18]

And what of the individual person's relation to God? Hinduism teaches that the essential self is naturally divine, and that the purpose of religion is to uncover the divinity within each of us. If a person clings to the illusive self, the ego, during life, his soul is condemned to reenter another body after death (reincarnation). The yogic exercises were designed to free us from the captivity of bodily illusion and lead us to blissful awareness of our oneness with Brahman, the eternal and absolute Reality. Strange as these beliefs are to our ways of thinking, even here we can find seeds of truth.

Genesis 1:26–27 tells us that God created men and women in His own image. Of course, having God's image is not the same as having God's nature or internal life. There is an infinite qualitative difference between Creator and creature. Wondrously made though we are,[19] divine we are not. Yet if we were to leave it at that, we would miss much of what Divine Revelation teaches about our union with God. For, far from denying that God's essence can dwell in human beings, Christianity views salvation as nothing less than being "divinized" in Christ by the gift of the Holy Spirit.[20] Through God's adoption of us by grace[21] bestowed at Baptism,[22] we are made indeed "partakers of the divine nature,"[23] sharers in the infinite splendor of God's life, though we remain personally distinct from God. In the great formula of Saint Athanasius and other early Church Fathers: God became

---

[17] George Weigel, *The Truth of Catholicism: Ten Controversies Explored* (New York: HarperCollins, 2001), p. 118.

[18] 1 John 4:8.

[19] Psalm 139:14.

[20] See Galatians 3:14.

[21] See Romans 8:14–16.

[22] See John 3:5; Acts 2:38; Titus 3:5–7.

[23] 2 Peter 1:4.

man so that man might become God. We therefore need not shy away from the idea of man as divine, provided we remember that divinization is the work of God's Spirit, not ours. We are joined to the Father by the Son, and we are joined to the Son by the Holy Spirit—in the sacraments and corporate life of the Church, and in the Spirit's sanctifying work within the soul.

Divinization, moreover, involves the body as well as the soul. On this point, the Hindu who practices yoga seems much like the Christian who kneels or fasts: both enlist the body in the service of the spirit. But whereas the Hindu desires to transcend bodily existence, the Christian does not. In Christian (and Jewish) tradition, the body is not a husk for the spiritual self but an integral part of a body-soul unity destined for eternal life with God in the company of the saints. The whole person, body and soul, will one day rise, when what is sown a physical body is raised a spiritual body,[24] conformed to Christ's glorified body.[25] Mary's bodily Assumption into Heaven—a doctrine affirmed by Catholics and, less dogmatically, by Orthodox Christians—anticipates the resurrection of all those whom Christ will save. This brings us to the interrelated doctrines of reincarnation and karma.

Hinduism teaches that the soul is given as many chances (incarnations) as needed to achieve awareness of its divinity, realization that *tat tvam asi*, "you are That [Brahman]," as the Upanishads say. Karma, the cumulative effect of our good and bad deeds, determines how we will be reincarnated after death.

Belief in reincarnation is incompatible with revealed truth: "It is appointed for men to die once, and after that comes judgment."[26] This statement needs to be considered within the broader context of the scriptural view of man as a totality of body, soul, and spirit destined to rise in glory.[27] Human beings get one temporal life, followed by eternal blessedness or damnation even before (so Catholics and most other Christians believe) bodily resurrection at the Last Day. That being noted, the law of karma and its attendant theory of reincarnation do contain seeds of the truth fully revealed in Christ and the Church.

---

[24] See 1 Corinthians 15:44.
[25] See Philippians 3:21.
[26] Hebrews 9:27.
[27] See, for example, Job 19:26 and 1 Corinthians 15:42–44.

Although most Hindus do not speak of sin in the biblical sense of the word, they, like Christians, believe that every human action has an effect on the soul for good or for ill. We are constantly determining our orientation toward God and others. Each time we consciously accept, or else reject, the attractions and repulsions that sway us, we build up our moral personality—or, as a Hindu might say, we work on our karma. We become what we do. And because our moral personality is not just a matter of bodily habits but of affections and habits of the soul as well, it will continue to exist after death in whatever state it was at the last moment of earthly life. In a very real sense, then, judgment goes on during this life and need not be repeated, but only manifested, after death.[28] God's judgment on us is simply a bringing to light of our moral personality, of what we have made of ourselves for eternity.

Hindus and Christians both profess union with God as requiring self-renunciation. For the Hindu, this means divesting the "unreal" personal self so to become one with the universal self or Atman, known as Brahman. For the Christian, it means putting off the old self[29] and "putting on Christ,"[30] which demands death to sin and life in conformity with God's will.[31] Scripture calls this the life of holiness or sanctification. But whereas Hinduism consigns the unenlightened soul to another embodiment, Catholicism teaches the existence of Purgatory for those who did not in this life achieve spiritual perfection or complete transformation in Christ. Those who die in the state of grace but are still burdened by residual sinfulness—selfishness, greed, vanity, and so on—must be thoroughly sanctified, fully purified of sin and its effects, before they can enjoy a Heaven of perfect love and communion with God.[32] The most pervasive and deadly sins, those of the spirit, are not cured merely by shedding our old bodies and receiving new ones. And while most Protestants repudiate the notion of Purgatory (for reasons to be explained later), all Christians agree that it is God's grace that elicits and enables our

[28] See John 3:18.
[29] See Ephesians 4:22.
[30] See Galatians 3:27.
[31] See Romans 6:11.
[32] See Revelation 21:27.

life in Christ every step of the way. Our moral efforts alone cannot save us. Only God can unite us to God.

Perhaps it was this intuition that gave rise to Hinduism's identification of Brahman with the Vedic gods—Vishnu, for example, who appeared in human form as Krishna. Might we see in this the innate human desire for a god who shares our lives and saves us from our misery? Was it not providential that such a development should take place in Hinduism at roughly the same time as Hebrew prophets and pagan sibyls were foretelling the coming of a godlike savior who would be born of the Jews? In any event, Hinduism's savior figures only appear to be human. Vishnu's "embodiment" is a far cry from the Incarnation of God the Son. No Hindu would say of Krishna what the Apostle Paul said of Jesus Christ: "in Christ God was reconciling the world to himself." [33]

We have found seeds of the Word very far from home. More often, however, we have found decisive obstacles to communion with the living God. Many elements of Hinduism are corrected, and not only fulfilled, by the light of the Gospel, like water changed into wine at Christ's command.

Buddhism

We turn our attention now to Hinduism's offshoot, Buddhism. Buddhism takes its name from the Sanskrit word *Buddha*, meaning Awakened One, a title used both to describe and venerate Siddhartha Gautama (*ca.* 563–483 B.C.), who was born in what is now the nation of Nepal.

Little is known about Siddhartha's life and personality. The common story is that he was a prince of the Shakya clan, whose family spared no effort to shield him from pain and suffering. Despite his family's precautions, Siddhartha encountered on four successive journeys what Buddhist folk tradition calls the "four passing sights." This legend made its way into Christianity, in the story of Saints Barlaam and Josaphat.[34] The first sight was an

---

[33] 2 Corinthians 5:19.

[34] During the Middle Ages, no legend was more famous throughout Christendom than the tale of Barlaam and Josaphat, nor were there many saints more beloved than its eponymous protagonists. Their joint feast, celebrated on

old man suffering all the infirmities of age; the second, a diseased man; the third, a corpse on a funeral pyre; and the fourth, a wandering beggar. Age, sickness, death, and want: How, Siddhartha mused, can people be spared these harsh realities? And so he set out on a journey, leaving behind his life of wealth and privilege—as well as his wife and child, according to some versions.

For a few years, Siddhartha lived and studied with Hindu ascetics, subsisting at times on just a few grains of rice per day. The extreme fasting nearly killed him. Realizing that the path of the ascetic was as pointless as that of the affluent, he sat under a Bo tree to meditate, determined not to rise until he had gained enlightenment. After weeks of meditation, during which he was subjected to a variety of visions and demonic temptations, Siddhartha realized the truth he had been seeking: one must choose the middle way between extreme austerity and luxury, the way of temperance, serenity, and personal responsibility. It was at this point that Siddhartha became the Buddha. Eager to share his newfound wisdom, he traveled from place to place preaching and recruiting disciples, the earliest of whom formed monastic communities.

The teachings of Siddhartha the Buddha, like those of Jesus the Christ, were passed on orally before being written down. Most of the sayings and sermons attributed to the Buddha are the product of later Buddhist teachers. Although little can reliably be said to be Siddhartha's actual words, there is general agreement as to his most basic doctrines.

Foremost among these teachings are the Four Noble Truths: (1) life is suffering; (2) the root of suffering is desire and attachment; (3) no desire means no suffering; and (4) desire can be overcome through following the Noble Eightfold Path.

The Noble Eightfold Path consists of three ways of practice: good conduct (right speech, right action, and right livelihood), mental development (right effort, right mindfulness, and right concentration), and wisdom (right understanding and right

---

November 27 in the West and August 26 in the East, was observed with a special relish by Christians of every place. Josaphat in particular was revered as the archetype of the holy prince, a child of royal blood who was willing to foreswear all the power and wealth of his earthly kingdom for the sake of the Kingdom of God.

thought). At first glance, this looks like a statement of the obvious. (Who wouldn't want to be right in all of these ways?) Their meaning, however, is not entirely self-evident. What, then, does each of these eight points mean?

Right speech means to avoid lying, harsh words, gossip, and idle talk. Right action means to avoid killing, stealing, and sexual misconduct. Right livelihood means to avoid any occupation that brings harm to others and ourselves, such as trading in lethal weapons, animals for slaughter (strict Buddhists are vegetarians), prostitution, and intoxicants. Right effort requires a constant struggle against all unwholesome thoughts and passions, such as greed, vengefulness, and lust. Right mindfulness means being aware of our true feelings and motives so to avoid enslavement to them. Right concentration aims to steady and calm the mind in order to realize the true nature of things; the object of our concentration may be our breathing, or a material thing such as a flower, or a concept such as compassion. Right understanding is accepting the Four Noble Truths. Finally, right thought means to avoid desire and ill will.

That, in brief, is the doctrine of the Four Noble Truths, Buddhism's answer to the question, How can we achieve liberation from suffering? There are other doctrines to consider, as well as Buddhism's sacred scriptures, religious rituals, and dominant forms. Suffice it to say, by way of preview, that Buddhism played in the history of South and East Asia something of the role of Christianity in the West, by effecting a reform or rather a complete overthrow of former paganism. In the process, some seeds of the Word were watered.

Nirvana: Blessed Nothingness

It is said that whenever the Buddha's disciples pressed him to go beyond the Four Noble Truths, he objected that any additional teaching would be superfluous—much as the first-century rabbi Hillel taught as the essence of Judaism: "What is hateful to you, do not do to others. That is the whole Torah [Law]; the rest is commentary." [35]

[35] *Talmud Bavli* (Babylonian Talmud), tractate *Shabbat* 31a.

What strikes us immediately is how unreligious Buddhism seems, at least in its original phase. Unlike the Hinduism from which it emerged, Buddhism does not speak of God (Brahman) or gods. It is silent about the origin of the universe, communion between the human and the Divine, an afterlife, and other subjects we normally associate with "religion." One of the parables attributed to the Buddha says that a concern about such things distracts us from our true dilemma. If you have been shot with a poisoned arrow, you do not ask for a description of the archer; you just want the arrow and poison out. Our everyday perceptions have been so disordered by our imprisonment in the world of illusion—a core Hindu idea, as we saw—that our first and most important task is to wake up.

Although the Buddha generally avoided theological and metaphysical questions, he was not silent about the soul. In fact, he taught the doctrine of *anatman* (Sanskrit for "no-soul"), thereby refuting Hindu belief in *atman*, the distinct self or "I" of a person. Earlier Indian tradition thought of *atman* as a spark that had become separated from the universal soul or Atman, known as Brahman (God); the deepest yearning of these sparks was to become reunited with their divine source. The Buddha rejected that way of thinking. What I think of as myself, he said, is not a single reality but a bundle of perceptions and sensations woven together for a limited time, without any underlying self, or soul. Just as a flame seems to be one thing but is in fact a continually burning set of gas molecules temporarily confined to one place, so the individual self or soul is merely a passing phenomenon.

In denying the reality of the human soul, the Buddha undercut the idea of reincarnation as traditionally understood in Hinduism. He likened reincarnation to lighting one candle from another: the second flame is caused by the first, but it is not the same flame. Since there is no personal identity or soul to begin with, nothing of substance passes from one body to another. Thus, in Buddhism, reincarnation is usually referred to as "transmigration."

Although Buddhism is atheistic, it does have an ultimate concern that orders all other concerns. The Buddhist's ultimate concern, the one that trumps all others, is liberation from suffering.

And because suffering stems from desire, salvation, for the Buddhist, means nirvana (from the Sanskrit *nibbati*, "to blow out"), an extinguishing of the flame of desire. Nirvana is the end of existence, an end to the cycle of birth and rebirth by becoming part of the flux of the universe. Yet, nirvana is not sheer nothingness. What are extinguished are illusion, want, and fear; what remains is the realm of the immortal, beyond words, but perfect bliss to all who attain it.

After death, one is either reborn into another body or enters nirvana. Only those who have attained enlightenment (buddhas) will reach the latter destination. Like the original Buddha, each individual must work out his own salvation. The Four Noble Truths show the way (*dharma*) to nirvana, but one must walk it alone. In computer terms, we program our own lives. The Buddha can teach us how to work with the keyboard, but he does not press the keys. What we get on the screen depends on our own skill, energy, and knowledge.

This focus on self-reliance, we will see, evolved in different directions as Buddhism developed and spread beyond India. After surveying the principal schools of Buddhist thought, we will search for bits and hints of the truth fully revealed in Christ and embodied in Catholicism.

Buddhism's Many Flavors

After the death of Gautama the Buddha in 483 B.C., his disciples tried to organize his teachings, or *dharma*, within a system of doctrines on which they could agree. These teachings were then orally passed down to future generations of monks within various Buddhist communities in India. In the first century B.C., scribes compiled the *dharma* on paper; these scriptures were written in Pali, a derivative of India's sacred language Sanskrit, and are known as the Pali Canon. The Pali Canon is also called the *Tipitaka* ("Three Baskets") because of its three parts: the Sutras, discourses of the Buddha; the Vinayas, ethical precepts and rules of monastic discipline; and the Abhidharmas, commentaries on the Sutras. Some traditions of later origin have also been recorded in Sanskrit.

Beginning around the second century B.C., Buddhism suffered

periods of fierce persecution in the land of its birth, first by Hindu rulers, later by invading Huns (nomadic Mongols), lastly by Muslims. After fifteen centuries, Buddhism was virtually wiped out from India. Nevertheless, it had already spread to other parts of Asia, absorbing local traditions along the way and developing many different schools and branches. Today most of the world's 375 million Buddhists follow either the Theravada or the Mahayana tradition.

Theravada (Pali for "the Way of the Elders") is the oldest surviving Buddhist tradition and predominates in Sri Lanka and most of Southeast Asia. It is intensely individualistic: each person must make his own arduous way to enlightenment, without the help of the gods or God. This is a fulltime work if taken seriously, and therefore best undertaken as a monk. Theravadins revere the Buddha as a great ethical teacher but do not venerate him as a god or savior, as do many Mahayana Buddhists.

Mahayana (Sanskrit for "Greater Vehicle," implying a better way to enlightenment than Theravada) is strongest in Nepal, China (including Tibet), Mongolia, Korea, Japan, and Vietnam. It is not a single group but a collection of sects: Tibetan, Pure Land, and Zen are all strands of the Mahayana tradition. Whereas Theravadins use the complete Tipitaka, Mahayana Buddhists rely mainly on the Sanskrit scriptures.

According to the Mahayana school, when the Buddha attained enlightenment, he did not enter nirvana but rather, moved by pity, returned to the people and helped others to reach nirvana. In contrast to the Theravada ideal of the *arhat*, the one who attains nirvana through self-effort, the Mahayana Buddhist strives to become a *bodhisattva*, one who forgoes entrance into nirvana so that he may remain in this world as long as there are creatures to be saved. The head monk of Tibetan Buddhism, the Dalai Lama, is believed to be the reincarnation of a past bodhisattva.

Zen Buddhism originated in China in the sixth century and spread from there to Korea and Japan. (*Zen* is the Japanese equivalent of *ch'an*, the Chinese pronunciation of the Sanskrit *dhyana*, "meditation.") Legend has it that one day the Buddha held up a flower and studied it for a long time without saying a word. A young disciple began to smile and the Buddha looked at him approvingly. Without hearing a word or studying scripture, the disciple gained enlightenment. Liberation, in Zen, is achieved not through words and concepts—Try describing color to a blind person—but through the profound realization, born of long hours in silent meditation, that one is already an enlightened being.

For those who cannot handle the subtleties of meditation, there is Pure Land Buddhism. This sect originated with the Japanese monk Honen (A.D. 1133–1212) who taught that most people, himself included, could not achieve liberation on their own, but only through the help of Amitabha, a bodhisattva who lived eons ago (Gautama spoke of him). Amitabha vowed that when he attained buddhahood, he would preside over a realm of ultimate bliss, the existence of which was revealed to him by his teacher, where there would be no evil and no obstacles to attaining nirvana. Honen taught that whoever invokes the name of the Buddha Amitabha with complete trust will, after death, be reborn in the Pure Land and thus much closer to nirvana.

Perhaps you have already detected in these various forms of Buddhism bits and premonitions of the truth fully revealed by God in Christ. Our task now is to identify these seeds of the Word and to spotlight their fullest flowering in the Catholic Church.

Buddhism and the Gospel

Paradoxically, it is precisely on those points where Buddhism and Christianity touch that we also find what most divides them. Buddhism's denial of the individual self or soul contradicts our most basic assumptions. A Christian could never accept that the self is unreal. On the contrary, we believe that there is something God loves that is myself and yourself, and that God wants this self, body and soul, to share in His own life. There is, however, a seed of truth present in the Buddhist doctrine of *anatman* ("no-soul"), and that is the recognition that what I regard as my true self may in fact be a deception. After all, what is the self? Is it the memory I have of myself, growing and changing? If so, would I cease to be myself after losing my memory to a stroke? Christian mystics have described their experience as one in which the self is seen, next to God, as nothing. Moreover, both Buddhism and

Christianity caution against self-deception in the spiritual life: someone may seem to be praying or acting selflessly when in fact he is indulging his own whimsy.

At the same time, our belief that human beings are created in the image of the triune God reminds us that our real self exists only in relationship. Just as the three Divine Persons love one another from all eternity, so it is in loving others and in being loved that our truest self emerges. The Buddhist seeks to extinguish the flame of desire because every desire, he believes, leads to a frustrating dead-end: "I want that" implies an "I" distinct from the "that," and this false distinction is the cause of suffering. The Christian goal, on the other hand, is not to extinguish the flame of desire but rather to convert it to a "flame of love" for God and for others. Our deepest longings are not absurd, but in one way or another find fulfillment in the God whose essence is love.

The ethical demands of Buddhism's Eightfold Noble Path are, for the most part, similar to those of Christian morality. We ought to abstain not only from evil deeds but also from evil desires. Buddhism's analysis of evil desires sheds light on the dynamics of violence, tackling the clinging to illusions (of superiority, for example) that lies at the root of violence. Yet the goal of moral uprightness for the Christian is not peace and detachment, but unselfish love in imitation of Christ. To the Buddhist, this is impossible: if the self is but an illusion, we cannot love another person for his own sake.

The motive of compassion for a Buddhist is not the welfare of the recipient but self-detachment, which leads to enlightenment. In spite of their doctrine, however, Buddhist experience often attests to a genuine love that is akin to Christian charity. Nevertheless, the Buddhist who wants to be wholly present to another human being must recognize and value the other's uniqueness. To embrace otherness is, paradoxically, to find oneself. As the perfect unity of the Trinity demonstrates, our relations are at the core of who we are.

Buddhism is very much attuned to the idea of suffering. The bodhisattva who wants to take upon himself all the sufferings of the world is the closest figure outside Christianity to that of the Suffering Servant in Isaiah, chapters 52–53. Christians believe that God has given us a definitive answer about suffering. This answer is not an abstract concept or idea but is embodied in Jesus Christ whom the prophets had foretold. By taking on flesh, the divine Son experienced suffering as a part of being human. Through the crucifixion, He willingly endured the painful reality of torture, clearly as a result of His own lack of selfish attachments. But the Cross is only half of the story.

The ultimate proof that self-emptying love is capable of conquering all suffering and evil is Christ's Resurrection from the dead. He did not allow the suffering He endured to detach Himself from the love He had for His heavenly Father and for all of humanity. Instead, He made suffering the vehicle by which He displayed the power of love over and above the power of suffering. And this, I believe, is the key to opening the doors of Buddhist hearts to the fullness of truth revealed by God. The Church has been given by her divine Founder the answers to the questions Buddhists have been seeking for more than two and a half millennia.

Confucianism

From Buddhism we turn to the religious philosophies of Confucianism and Taoism. Besides Zen Buddhism, which spread from China to Japan and Korea, Confucianism and Taoism are typically Chinese worldviews. It is tempting for Westerners to treat Buddhism, Confucianism, and Taoism as if these were rigidly separate schools of belief. On the contrary, they have strongly influenced one another and are all deemed part of a common pool of wisdom. We can, however, make a rough division of labor: Buddhism deals with suffering, Confucianism with morality, and Taoism with our place in the universe.

For most of China's long history, Confucianism was the guiding philosophy for the state and for the lives of families and individuals. Confucius (the Latinized version of K'ung Fu-tzu, "Grand Master K'ung") lived from 551 to 479 B.C. and is reputed to have been the most learned man of his time. Born in the small feudal state of Lu (today Shantung Province) from a noble but poor family, he lost his father early on. He married at a young age but soon divorced. Having worked as a police magistrate and perhaps as a minister of justice and statesman, he became an itinerant teacher, traveling throughout China with disciples. Second-generation disciples compiled the master's sayings in a volume known as the *Lun yü*, translated into English as the *Analects of Confucius*.

Confucius never claimed to be divine, inspired, or even good. Only one quality did he claim: "The unwearying effort to learn [not abstract knowledge but self-improvement] and unflagging patience in teaching others."[36] And although he discouraged speculation about spirits and the afterlife, it would be mistaken to view Confucianism as a wholly ethical system with no hint of the supernatural. Learning about morality for Confucius meant learning about the will of "Heaven" (*T'ien*), and the *Analects* give ample evidence that Confucius understood Heaven as a deity with a personal nature. No human being truly knows him, but only Heaven; true happiness depends on the approval of Heaven rather than human praise, on interior qualities rather than external things; Heaven begot the moral force in him, and this force is available to all people even if most don't avail themselves of it. Furthermore, in the teachings of the great Confucian disciple Meng-tzu (371–289 B.C.), known in the West as Mencius, "Heaven" appears to be just another name for God.

Anyone wishing to follow the way of Heaven must develop his *Te*, the inner moral power or virtue bestowed by Heaven on all people. Growth in virtue is the goal of all learning and indeed of all human endeavors: to become ethically perfect is to become fully human. So virtue, rather than stifling human freedom, unfolds human potential. Yet Confucius said he never knew anyone, including himself, who has reached the pinnacle of moral perfection, which he described as *Jen*, translated either as "full humanity" or "goodness." Nor did he know whether even those without vanity, resentment, or greed would qualify for *Jen*. He could only say that whoever obtains *Jen* would never be unhappy.

The person who lives by the ideal of *Jen* is a *Chün-tzu*, "superior man." The *Chün-tzu* always seeks what is right, even if he gains nothing by it; he stands in awe of Heaven's ordinances;

---

[36] *Analects* 7:33.

he calls attention to the good qualities in others, not to their defects; he is dignified but never haughty; he appreciates education, the arts, and music; he studies not to impress others but for self-improvement; his moral force influences even his superiors; and he is so reliable that if you should entrust to him either an orphan or the welfare of a state, he would prove competent and trustworthy.

Personal virtue naturally benefits society. Confucius taught that order in one's personal life leads to order within the family; order within the family leads to order within the village, and so on up to the state and the whole world. Is this merely human wisdom, or is it an intuition of what the incarnate God of Heaven said, some centuries later, about faithfulness in small matters being a sure test of faithfulness in great ones? [37]

Human culture accumulated many lofty moral teachings, and the sayings of Confucius certainly belong to its best. Hardly any moral advice of Confucius needs to be discarded when one embraces Christianity. In fact, almost all of it should be followed. Perhaps no other non-Christian moral teaching comes so close to what the Catholic tradition calls the "natural moral law," that is, the rule of right and wrong, of good and evil, rooted in human nature, which every mature person, regardless of religious belief or lack thereof, can know by use of his God-given reason.

If there are obvious differences between Christian and Confucian morality, it is largely because the new "law of love" proclaimed in the Gospels fulfils and perfects the natural moral law. Confucius did not teach, as Jesus taught, that we should love our enemies, or that we are called to share in God's own love for our fellow human beings.

Consider, too, the high value both Confucianism and Christianity place on friendship, as exemplified in the former by the *Chün-tzu*, "superior man." Christianity elevates friendship to a supernatural level, realized in the Christian virtue of charity. By having Christ's friendship, a Christian can love all people as Christ does, even if he is not understood and loved by them. Moreover, a Christian not only makes friends for himself but also causes others to be friends with each other. Our natural capacity

[37] See Luke 16:10–12.

for friendship is greatly enlarged by faith in Jesus Christ and union with Him.

For Confucius, man's highest goal was the cultivation of *Jen*, "full humanity." Jen occupies the same position in Confucianism as charity does in Christianity: it is the queen of all virtues and the bond of perfection. To attain *Jen* requires the conscientious performance of one's duties toward Heaven (*T'ien*), toward oneself, and toward others. Filial piety—loyalty and devotion to one's parents, elderly relatives, and ancestors—is, for Confucius, *Jen*'s starting point.

In later Confucian tradition, however, filial piety so dominated Chinese culture that it became for many people the very meaning of life. It is on this point that Christianity provides a necessary corrective. Filial piety becomes idolatrous if it is not offset by the idea of human brotherhood under God's Fatherhood. The teaching of Jesus Christ brings filial duty back into balance.[38] Christians, while likewise emphasizing family-centered living, do not (or should not) make a god of the family head, or allow familial relations to degenerate into what an eminent Chinese convert to Catholicism, John C. H. Wu (1899–1986), described as the "detestable clannishness, from which China has suffered so much."[39] Enlightened by Christ, filial piety is not the central theme of *Jen* but rather its first stage, and *Jen* itself is made subordinate to that higher filial piety which we owe to God the Father of all.

Although the Confucian concept of *Jen* adds nothing to Christianity, it can serve as a reminder to modern Christians of the Fourth Commandment, which, as Saint Paul pointed out, is the first commandment with a promise.[40] The extreme individualism that characterizes modern Western culture has eclipsed this important precept in the lives of many Christians.

An old Confucian scholar's reaction to the Catholic wedding of John Wu's eldest son provides a memorable testimony to Confucianism's capacity for Christ. He was so deeply impressed by the ceremonies of the Nuptial Mass that he remarked, "This is

[38] See, for example, Luke 14:26.

[39] John A. Lindblom, "John C. H. Wu and the Evangelization of China," *Logos: A Journal of Catholic Thought and Culture* 8:2 (2005) 130–164, at p. 146. Baptized in 1937, Wu was appointed China's ambassador to the Vatican in 1947.

[40] See Ephesians 6:2–3.

exactly what our old marital rites had foreshadowed!" In other words, the seeds that Confucianism had sown came into flowering in the Christian Sacrament of Holy Matrimony, where human love and family solidarity are ordered to the supernatural love of God and perfected by His grace.

China's ancient system of dynastic rule was based on the Confucian system of values. So when the last dynasty, the Ch'ing, fell in 1911, Confucianism soon lost its place as the dominant philosophy. After the Communist revolution of 1949, the government tried to erase whatever remained of Confucian thought from the nation's consciousness. Much has changed since then. In the wake of the complete collapse of Communist ideology and the resulting lack of any strong moral foundation capable of filling the godlike role that Communism once claimed for itself, officials have been encouraging the resurgence of Confucian values.

This bodes well for the cause of Christ. As Monsignor Fulton Sheen said so well in the foreword to John Wu's spiritual autobiography *From Confucius to Christ*: "The distance from nature to grace, from sin to salvation, from doubt to faith, is the same for a Western soul as for the Eastern soul, for only Christ's grace can bridge the distance. From this perspective, Confucius can be just as good a starting point for the discovery of Our Divine Lord as Aristotle."[41]

Taoism

Taoism takes its name and inspiration from the *Tao-te Ching* ("The Book of the Way and Its Power"), a collection of Chinese verse traditionally attributed to Lao-tzu ("Old Master"), who was possibly a contemporary of Confucius. Its 81 short, numbered stanzas contain many paradoxes such as "He who knows does not speak, and he who speaks does not know" (no. 56) and "Truly, one may gain by losing; and one may lose by gaining" (no. 42). First translated into Latin by Jesuit missionaries in 1788, no other book except the Bible has been translated so often. Because Taoism is often entwined with Buddhism and traditional folk religions, it is hard to know the number of its adherents.

[41] "Introduction" to John C. H. Wu, *From Confucianism to Catholicism*, trans. Marlette Wickes (Huntington, Ind.: Our Sunday Visitor Press, 1949), p. 4.

Central to Taoism is a belief in *Tao* (pronounced "dow"), usually translated as "the Way." Eternal, invisible, and unfathomable, Tao is the origin of all creation, the force that lies behind the functions and changes of nature. All things are connected and unified in Tao. It is tempting to equate Tao, so described, with the "immortal, invisible, only God"[42] in whom "all things hold together."[43] But Tao is more like Hinduism's Brahman: an impersonal "it" that cannot be prayed to. The opening line of the *Tao-te Ching* warns the reader off any attempt to pin down the supreme Reality with human concepts and language: "The Tao that can be expressed is not the eternal Tao." We may compare Saint John Chrysostom's doctrine that a comprehended "God" is no God at all.[44]

Tao generates *ch'i* ("breath"), the constantly moving energy found in all things, as well as the two opposite but complementary forces of *yin* and *yang*. Yin is the feminine, dark, earthly, and passive principle in nature; yang is the masculine, light, heavenly, and active principle. Lao-tzu advised a preference for yin: "Know the masculine but keep to the feminine. . . . Know the white but keep to the black. . . . Know the glorious but keep to the lowly" (no. 28).

Harmony results when yin and yang form a whole. Taoism's most recognized emblem, a circle encasing rolling waves of black and white, represents the idealized harmony of these two forces: within the black wave rides a white dot, and, conversely, the white wave contains a black dot. The intertwined halves within the yin-yang circle represent all opposites: hot and cold, loss and gain, health and sickness, constancy and change, and so on. Neither makes sense without the other.

Whereas Confucianism focuses on the individual as a member of society, Taoism would have us turn away from society and seek freedom in the wordless contemplation of nature's wonders. The Taoist ideal is to live naturally, allowing things to exist and develop without interference or conflict. And the way to do this is *wu-wei* ("not doing"), which means something like letting things take their course. This is not to suggest that people should

---

[42] 1 Timothy 1:17.

[43] Colossians 1:17.

[44] See John Chrysostom's series of homilies *On the Incomprehensible Nature of God* (delivered over a period of several years beginning in A.D. 386), esp. iii and iv.

spend their time doing nothing, in idle meditation, but rather that their activities should fit into the natural pattern of things and not be driven by ambition, excessive desire, or pride.

Taoists often use the example of a river as a lesson for how to live. A river is constant yet ever changing, and over time can wear down the mightiest rocks. So too should people seek out those things that are eternal, yet always be open to spontaneity and change. In other words, "Go with the flow."

Although Taoism does not recognize an omnipotent Being beyond the cosmos, it nevertheless has many gods, most of them borrowed from other cultures. These deities are within this universe and are themselves subject to Tao, the impersonal "mother of all things." At the heart of Taoist ritual is the attempt to bring order and harmony to nature, society, and individuals. Recognizing that physical actions have spiritual effects, Taoism regards yoga, meditation, and martial arts as important activities.

Temple rituals are used to regulate *ch'i* and balance the flow of yin/yang both for individuals and the wider community. One such ritual involves each household in a village bringing an offering for the local deities. A Taoist priest dedicates the offerings on behalf of the families, asks the gods to bring peace and prosperity to the village, and performs an elaborate rite of cosmic renewal.

Because Taoism thrives on paradox and mystification, it is not easy for practical Western minds to comprehend. Yet the enigmatic sayings of Lao-tzu, especially those concerning the mystery of Tao, afford fascinating glimpses of the fullness of truth revealed in Jesus Christ.

Taoism and the Gospel: Christ, the Way-Word-Son

Of all the ancient sages, it seems none came closer than Lao-tzu to knowing all that can be known about God without the help of Divine Revelation. His understanding of Tao ("the Way") could well describe what the ancient Greek philosophers called the *Logos* ("word" or "reason"), that is, the underlying cause and ordering pattern of all being—the Intelligence behind intelligent design.

Saint John the Evangelist, who was familiar with Greek philosophy by the time he wrote his Gospel, declares that what the philosophers had long sought after—the *Logos*—became flesh in Jesus of Nazareth: "In the beginning was the Word [*Logos*], and the Word was with God, and the Word was God ... all things were made through him.... And the Word became flesh and dwelt among us."[45] So the Christian tradition, starting with the prologue to John's Gospel, identifies the uncreated Word of God with Jesus Christ. It is only natural, therefore, that Christian missionaries would try to explain the Incarnation to Chinese minds by describing Jesus as the eternal Tao made flesh.

Yet, as we saw, Lao-tzu did not think of Tao as a personal being (never mind one who assumed a human body!), although he did verge on this understanding in attributing to Tao personal characteristics such as benevolence. Nonetheless, Taoism and Christianity have vastly different underlying visions of reality. Whereas the God of Genesis speaks the universe into existence by a personal act of the will (through the agency of the Word/Son, so Christians believe), Tao creates impersonally, dividing itself into the many visible things by way of begetting: "Tao begets One; one begets two; two begets three; three begets all things."[46] Perhaps this passage expresses an inkling of the Trinity, but in the end Taoism's god remains but a force that neither creates beings in its own image nor freely calls them to itself.

How does one live by Tao? Obedience to Tao strongly resembles obedience to what the Western philosophical tradition calls the natural law. In fact, the great Christian apologist C. S. Lewis used "the Tao" as a shorthand term for natural law. Put simply, "natural law" refers to the moral order in the warp and woof of creation: those permanent moral truths built into the nature of man and knowable by reason. For example, it is against the natural law, and not only Divine Revelation, to engage in homosexual acts or intentionally to destroy innocent human life. Identifying natural law with Tao presents an evangelical opportunity for Christians. Telling a modern-day pagan that he has disobeyed God's Word is likely to have little effect; but telling

[45] John 1:1–14.
[46] *Tao-te Ching*, 42.

44

him that he has, in Taoist terms, gone "against the grain of the universe" might pack more rhetorical punch, especially if the inevitability of cosmic splinters is spelled out.

Even apart from natural law, there is much to be said for the Taoist who lives "naturally" so as to be one with Tao. It is the wise, after all, who accommodate themselves to reality. They attempt their harvests in season. They tear along the perforated line. Whether they get their wisdom from books, or from their grandmother, or simply from observing life, the wise eventually learn and then live by such truths as these: The more you talk, the less people listen; —if your word is no good, people will not trust you; —envy of fat cats does not make them slimmer and will rot your bones; —if you scratch certain itches, they just itch more.

And as for scriptural wisdom, Christian phrases such as "Blessed are the meek," "He who wishes to save his life must lose it," and "When I am weak, then I am strong" have nearly identical counterparts in the *Tao-te Ching*. These are further evidence of Spirit-sown "seeds of the Word" preparing pagan cultures for the revelation of Christ.

Consider, too, Lao-tzu's preference for *yin*, the "feminine" aspect of nature. Two examples of *yin* are water, which always seeks its lowest level, from which it gives life, and infancy, which epitomizes lowliness. Christ was born of a woman and showed typically feminine tenderness on many occasions, including His motherly lament over Jerusalem.[47] He is the "living water" flowing through the depths of the soul and "welling up to eternal life."[48] And though He was divine, He humbled Himself by taking on flesh, literally becoming a baby and later suffering a humiliating execution.[49]

In the light of faith, the teachings of Confucius and Lao-tzu concerning Heaven, the Way, and Goodness—*T'ien, Tao, Jen*—point to the divine Trinity of Father, Son, and Spirit of Love—the God revealed in Jesus Christ.

---

[47] See Matthew 23:37.
[48] John 4:14.
[49] See Philippians 2:6–8.

Summary

Thus far we have explored Hinduism, Buddhism, Confucianism, and Taoism, in that order. All are outgrowths of Asian cultures, and all have greatly influenced the development of those cultures.

Hinduism and Buddhism originated in India, although Buddhism has long been virtually extinct in its native land and is practiced primarily in the Far East. Both religions focus on escaping the cycle of reincarnation or rebirth by achieving enlightenment, yet there is no one commonly accepted path to that end. Moreover, both religions view the experience of the divine as the loss of one's personhood, either by realizing one's innate divinity (Hinduism) or by allowing oneself to pass into the extinction of nirvana (Buddhism).

Confucianism and Taoism began in China and spread to those Asian countries influenced by Chinese culture, particularly Korea and Japan. In some ways these religions are more akin to philosophy than to religion as it is understood in the West. Confucianism deals with human relationship and Taoism deals with life in harmony with nature.

The fact that Eastern religions defy easy classification is illustrated by the quip, "Zen is Taoism disguised as Buddhism."[50] Many Chinese families would see no contradiction in celebrating a Confucian coming-of-age ceremony, calling in a Taoist priest to bless the start of a business venture, and opting for a Buddhist funeral.

We noted Hinduism's bewildering variety of forms. Brahman is described as the Universal Soul that permeates all things, but is also conceived in later Hindu tradition as having three personal forms: Brahma the creator, Vishnu the preserver, and Shiva the destroyer, with Vishnu taking human form as Krishna. Thus we found Hindu intimations of the tri-personal God whose Second Person, the Son, became man. At the same time, mainstream Hinduism's belief that all things are ultimately identical with Brahman—a belief firmly rooted in the Upanishadic scriptures—is at odds with the biblical distinction between the Creator God

---

[50] Ray Grigg, *The Tao of Zen* (Boston: Charles E. Tuttle, 1994), p. xiii.

and creation. In addition, where there is a sort of incarnation in Hinduism, it is God disguised as human, not God as truly human while remaining divine.

We found a premonition of the Savior in the Buddhist *bodhisattva* (enlightened one) who, in compassion for the world, refuses to enter nirvana until all sentient beings have been liberated. Apart from this, Buddhism knows no God. Buddhism's "traditional" branch, the Theravada, regards the desire for personal immortality and for continued human relationships as misplaced. The doctrine of *anatman* ("no-self") says that there is no individual self, or soul, who could relate to a God; nor is it possible to think or say anything about the ultimate Reality. Where a God-concept has developed in Buddhism, it is generally some impersonal "Buddha-nature."

The teachings of Confucius and Lao-tzu often coincide with what the Apostle Paul calls the "law written on the heart" [51] and what classical Western philosophy calls the natural law, meaning those abiding truths embedded in human nature and human action. Like Hinduism and Buddhism, Confucianism and Taoism do not recognize a personal God who enjoins us to imitate Himself,[52] and still less a God whose gift of grace raises us to a share in His divine life.[53] Consequently, the practice of virtue often degenerates into a self-sufficient quest for immortality, either spiritual or physical, through meditation, breathing exercises, and various kinds of esoteric superstition. Yet Chinese religion is aware of a transcendent power, *T'ien* (Heaven), at work in those who seek *Jen* (goodness) by following the *Tao* (Way)—fragmentary glimpses, perhaps, of the heavenly Father whose Spirit elicits and sustains our union with Christ, the Incarnate Way.

But enough of pagan wisdom, real or imagined. It is time to leave our contemplations, as the Magi left theirs, for the brighter visions that beam afar.[54] We shall now move westward, as it were, into the three great monotheistic religions whose birthplace is the Near East: Judaism, Christianity, and Islam. All three

---

[51] See Romans 2:15.

[52] See Leviticus 19:2; Matthew 5:48.

[53] See 2 Peter 1:4.

[54] "Sages, leave your contemplations, Brighter visions beam afar; Seek the great Desire of nations, Ye have seen His natal star": from stanza 3, "Angels, from the Realms of Glory," by James Montgomery (1771–1854).

religions trace their origins back to a definitive revelation in history, and give us a picture of God and the world in obvious contrast to what we have seen thus far.

III

NON-CHRISTIAN MONOTHEISM

JEWS, Christians, and Muslims (as the followers of Islam are called) constitute nearly 40 percent of the world's population. While there are deep religious differences among the three groups, they have enough in common to come under one heading.

First, all three religions are strictly monotheistic, meaning they profess one God who created the world and manifests Himself in it, but is distinct from His creation. By contrast, the Asian religions we have studied thus far admit of polytheism (many gods), pantheism (all is God or a part of God), a blend of polytheism and monotheism (one God under the form of many personal gods), and even atheism (no God at all).

Second, these monotheistic religions, unlike the religions of India and East Asia, trace their origins back to a definitive revelation of God in history. Jews claim that revelation culminated in Moses. Christians confess Jesus of Nazareth as the final and definitive revelation of God. Muslims hold that Muhammad is God's greatest and last prophet. At the core of each religion is a body of sacred scriptures believed to be the revealed Word of God and used for religious orientation, spiritual enrichment, and communal education. Jews and Christians seek authority from the Bible, which for Jews consists of the Tanakh (what Christians call the Old Testament) and for Christians comprises the Old and New Testaments. Islam's holy book is the Qur'an (also spelled Koran).

Third, the foundation of these three religions is a personal encounter with the living God who makes Himself known and calls people into relationship with Him. In Eastern religion, especially the non-dualist form of Hinduism, God and the world are identical, and the experience of God is seen as the disappearance of one's personhood into the impersonal Absolute, like a drop of water in wine. Cardinal Joseph Ratzinger (now Pope Benedict

XVI), in his superbly lucid book *Truth and Tolerance*, describes the contrast as the "unity of merging, with its tendency to eliminate identity" versus a "unity of love [that] is higher than formless identity."[55]

Jews, Christians, and Muslims have a fundamental disagreement about the nature and actions of God. Naturally, the question arises: Do Christians, Jews, and Muslims worship the same God? The revelation of God as Father—a truth which Jesus recalled to the minds of His fellow Israelites—is, for Christians, not simply a metaphor for God's providential care of His people.[56] It says something also about the divine essence, that is, God as He is in Himself. Saint Athanasius insisted that God as Father cannot be conceived apart from a Son; therefore, a deity whose interior life lacks the relation of sonship is not the God revealed by Jesus Christ. It seems to follow that the answer to the question posed is no. But to conclude that Jews, Christians, and Muslims worship different Gods would put us on our way to embracing the first great heresy in the Church: Marcionism, named after the second-century priest who taught that the God of the Old Testament is not the God whom Jesus called Father but a fickle, despotic lawgiver whose rule Jesus came to overthrow.

Happily, there is another way of looking at it, one that affirms the truth of God's nature as revealed by Christ while acknowledging both Christianity's and Islam's indebtedness to the Hebrew Scriptures. Father Richard John Neuhaus has captured it nicely:

> Christians confess that there is one God—Father, Son, and Holy Spirit. Jews worship the one God whom Jesus called Father and taught us to worship, although Jews do not recognize that the God whom we both worship has revealed himself as Father, Son, and Holy Spirit. Muslims worship the same God (although calling him Allah, as do Arabic-speaking Jews and Christians), believing that His definitive revelation was given through Muhammad....

[55] Joseph Ratzinger, *Truth and Tolerance: Christian Belief and World Religions*, trans. Henry Taylor (San Francisco: Ignatius Press, 2004), p. 47

[56] See, for example, Hosea 11:1.

The dispute between Jews, Muslims, and Christians is not over whether they worship the same God, but over how the one God is rightly understood and worshiped.[57]

With reservations, then, let us accept the premise that, despite all that divides them, Christians, Jews, and Muslims worship the same God—the God who, four thousand years ago, called Abraham to be a blessing to the nations.

Judaism

The followers of the three great monotheistic religions—Judaism, Christianity, and Islam—are collectively called the "children of Abraham" because all three religions trace their origins to this patriarch from Mesopotamia. Judaism, the oldest of these religions, numbers more than 13 million adherents.

According to tradition, four thousand years ago the one true God called Abram, later renamed Abraham, and told him: "Go from your country and your kindred and your father's house to the land that I will show you. And I will make of you a great nation, and I will bless you, and make your name great, so that you will be a blessing. I will bless those who bless you, and him who curses you I will curse; and by you all the families of the earth shall be blessed."[58] Abraham and his followers, in return for their faith and devotion, were to be a people who would have a special relationship with God.

Descendants of Abraham's grandson Jacob, later renamed Israel, founded twelve tribes known as the "Children of Israel" or Israelites. They settled in Canaan (present-day Lebanon and Israel/Palestine), until a famine drove them to Egypt, where they apparently prospered until the pharaohs enslaved them.

Several centuries after Abraham, Moses led the Israelites out of bondage in Egypt. They wandered the Sinai Peninsula on their way back to Canaan, the land that God had promised to Abraham and his descendants. It was during this period that God revealed Himself as *Yahweh* (Hebrew for "I am Who am") and

[57] Richard John Neuhaus, "While We're at It," *First Things* 140 (February 2004): 72.

[58] Genesis 12:1–3.

gave Moses the Ten Commandments at Mount Sinai. The Commandments and other God-given laws established the principles and beliefs of God's Chosen People. They are written in the Torah (Hebrew for "law" or "teaching"), also called the Pentateuch—the first five books of the Bible. From Sinai the Israelites invaded Canaan and conquered its cities.

To the south lived their most formidable foe, the Philistines. Battles against the Philistines turned in Israel's favor under three powerful kings: Saul, David, and Solomon. King David united the many tribes into the nation of Israel. His heir, Solomon, built great palaces and the first Temple in the capital city of Jerusalem, and Israel became a political power. The Israelites observed their religion mostly as animal and grain sacrifices offered in the Temple.

When Solomon died, the kingdom divided into two parts: Israel in the north, with Samaria as its capital, and Judah in the south, with its capital Jerusalem. The northern segment fell to the Assyrians in 721 B.C. In 587 B.C., the smaller southern kingdom succumbed to the Babylonians, who destroyed Solomon's Temple and took many of Judah's leading families away to Babylonia (present-day Iraq).

Though scattered to other lands and with no more Temple for divine service, many of these exiled Judean families held fast to Judaism, as their religion would come to be named, through weekly gatherings ("synagogues" in Greek) where teachers, or rabbis, read and explained Sacred Scripture. Even after the Persian king Cyrus II (the Great) conquered Babylonia in 539 B.C. and allowed the exiled Jews to return to their homeland, many Jews continued worshiping in synagogues, thus paving the way for an observance of Judaism apart from the Temple. Construction of a second Temple was completed in 515 B.C.; this was greatly enlarged in the first century B.C. under Herod but destroyed by the Romans in A.D. 70.

Abraham's vocation marks a certain beginning of God's plan of salvation, and Israel was very conscious of her special part in that mystery. Not through her own virtue but by God's free election, Israel would be the first to enjoy the blessings of salvation. In turn, Israel would be the means of bringing salvation to the rest of the world.

But God's saving plan did not take its absolute beginning with Abraham. The Apostle Paul insists on this more than once when he writes about Abraham's place in the divine plan. God's will to save, as it has been revealed in the Bible, is pushed back to the very beginning, to the first rejection of God's goodness by the sin of Adam in which all human beings are implicated. Man rejected God's invitation to intimate union with Himself. But God's intention was not irreparably frustrated, for in Genesis 3:15 we see the first hint of the good news about our salvation. With this as a background, the call of Abraham brings up the curtain on the great religious drama of Israel and humanity. Forces are here and now set in motion that would lead to man's reconciliation with the God who calls and commands.

The Chosen People

Around 1250 B.C., God delivered the Israelites, Abraham's descendants through his son Isaac, from slavery in Egypt, and this motley throng was forged into a nation at the foot of Mount Sinai. This is the beginning of it all, as recounted in the Book of Exodus: the flight from Egypt, the crossing of the Red Sea, the march into the desert, the gathering at Sinai. And through it all, there was the presence of God, "the pillar of cloud by day and the pillar of fire by night." [59] It was His mighty arm and outstretched hand that freed Israel, and it was His voice that sounded in the thunder on the mountain, summoning their leader Moses to hear His words.

This was Israel's first encounter with the true God. This was the moment of Israel's birth as God's "Chosen People" whose true freedom would consist in serving God. "For to me the sons of Israel are servants, they are my servants whom I brought forth out of the land of Egypt: I am the Lord your God." [60] Above all, this initial encounter with God etched in the people's consciousness the kind of God He is. First, God *is*. So basic is this idea, but so peculiarly Israel's, that it is enshrined in the name of God given to Moses: *Yahweh*, "I am Who am," a name connected with

[59] Exodus 13:22.
[60] Leviticus 25:55.

the Hebrew verb *hayah*, "to be." Not a particularly descriptive name, that. Other people in those days had names for their gods—Ra, Amon, Moloch, Baal—and people knew what those names meant. But that's precisely the point. To name something is to pin it down, to bring it within your grasp. The God of Israel is not one to be captured in images or in names. Moses asked God His name because he wanted to instruct the people about the God who rescued them in terms they could understand. A name would put Israel's God in the same category as other gods and at the same time distinguish Him from them: "They have Moloch but we have . . ." And God answered, in effect: "No! It is enough for you to know that I am."

Although the biblical God is beyond our grasp, He is not remote and impersonal. On the contrary, it is because He is that He acts, and it is in His action that He shows Himself and that we come into contact with Him. Pagan gods have names but little else, as the psalmist says: "They have mouths but they speak not; they have eyes but they see not; they have ears but they hear not; nor is there any breath in their mouths."[61] Yahweh, on the other hand, really exists and really acts, and in those actions He is known. He exists eternally above and outside human affairs, yet governs all according to His immutable will.

For the first time, then, the people had come into contact with a God who is not the product of human hands or minds but is totally Other. Even so, He must have been with Israel all along, as His first words to Moses imply: "I am the God of Abraham, Isaac, and Jacob."[62] The God of Sinai is the God of those long-dead ancestors. It was therefore not a question of a little desert tribe and its god, as other nations had their gods. Israel's God is the God of all time and all peoples.

Naturally, not all of this would be immediately clear. What was clear from the start was that the God of Israel is God alone. But why should He bother with the descendants of Abraham? The only possible answer was mindboggling: "It was not because you were the largest of all nations . . . but because the Lord loves you and is keeping the oath which He swore to your fathers."[63]

[61] Psalm 135:16–17.
[62] Exodus 3:6.
[63] Deuteronomy 7:7–8.

Therefore, the God beyond all names must be a *good* God—kind, merciful, and loving—even if also a jealous God who forbids the worship of false gods.[64]

The Israelites' first divine encounter determined not only their concept of God but also their notion of themselves. Second only to monotheism in importance was the conviction that God had chosen Israel as His own people to bear His revelation to the world. Let us now consider this privileged relationship.

A Covenantal People

A people had come into being at the foot of Mount Sinai. Just as surely as the Israelites could look to Yahweh as their supreme Lord, so He would look on them as His Chosen People, picked out, set apart. This involved obligations as well as privileges, and above all the obligation to complete loyalty, to single-minded service of their God: "You shall have no other gods besides me."[65] The relationship between God and Israel is expressed throughout the Bible in the single word "covenant."

The next stage was for this people to acquire a homeland. Just north of the desert where they wandered was the land of Canaan, later named Palestine, which their ancestors had once entered in obedience to God's call.[66] And so, to Canaan they turned. The Israelites had to fight their way through hostile peoples up to the borders of Canaan, and then face the Canaanites who lived there. And all the time, if they did carve out a stretch of land for themselves, they were a prey to the Ammonites and Midianites and other nomadic tribes in search of booty.

Most of all, there were the Philistines who had arrived to this land at roughly the same time as Israel and with the same aim: possession. For the next two centuries, warfare was Israel's normal way of life. In their struggle, the same faith as they had found at Sinai was the determining factor. They were God's people, and so their struggle was God's struggle and their enemies were God's enemies. Their leader in battle was God Himself, symbolized by the Ark of the Covenant containing the

[64] See Exodus 20:3; Deuteronomy 5:7.
[65] Exodus 20:3.
[66] See Genesis 12:4–9.

Commandments inscribed on stone tablets and other sacred items. Their victory or defeat depended on their faithfulness to Yahweh. This favor was shown often in great signs, as recounted in the Book of Joshua: crossing the Jordan dryshod into Canaan through a miraculous stoppage of the river, the falling of the walls of Jericho, the sun standing still for Joshua.[67] Moreover, the goal for which they struggled was not merely a homeland but the land God had promised them.[68] It was their "inheritance," and by winning this inheritance, God's promises to Abraham and his descendants would be fulfilled.

Israel owed its national existence to God: it was He who brought them out of Egypt, who gave the Law by which their life was to be regulated, and who gave them victory over their foes. These three great events, more than anything else, shaped the Israelites' understanding of God. The God who makes His will known (the Law) is the same God who saves His people *from* something (the Exodus) *for* something (the Promised Land). But *why* did God freely choose Israel and espouse her as His own possession?

The Bible provides us a clue by extending the term "covenant" to men who were faithful to God long before Israel came to be, to Noah for instance,[69] or by means of genealogies: Abraham is linked with Noah, and Noah with Adam, and even with "the genealogy of heaven and earth."[70] Though the facts are lost in the mists of prehistory, the meaning is plain: Israel's encounter with God at Sinai does not form an isolated moment in history that might well come to an end, as other nations had appeared for a while and then vanished along with their gods. Israel is part of a divine plan, and her past holds the key to understanding her present and future.

By putting the account of Adam's sin at the beginning of the story of salvation, the inspired author makes it the context for all the rest he has to say: the troubled history of the world, the catastrophic flood, the call of Abraham, the choice of Israel—all this is connected with the ultimate victory over evil promised

---

[67] See, respectively, Joshua 3:9–17; 6:12–27; 10:9–15.
[68] See Genesis 13:14–15; 15: 18–21; 17:8.
[69] See Genesis 6:18.
[70] Genesis 2:4.

in Genesis 3:15. We might say that the Israelites lived by two articles of faith, both of which explain the hope that sustained them during their long and troubled history. First, the one true God had intervened in their past, above all in the great event of the Exodus. Second, God would intervene again at a time of His own choosing. The breadth of that hope and its pervasive influence on Judaism are our next concern.

The Hope of Israel

We have been speaking of Israel as a people, a nation. For the first few centuries of its existence, however, this "nation" was no close-knit social organization but rather a federation of tribes bound together by a common covenant with Yahweh their God, who delivered them from Egypt and led them safely through the Red Sea into the Sinai Desert. This tribal structure was a big handicap during and after Israel's struggle to attain the promised land of Canaan. And so, around 1050 B.C., the tribes of Israel united under one leader, a king.

Saul was their first. When he proved unsatisfactory, they found another to succeed him: David, whose story is told in the two books of Samuel and in the first two chapters of the First Book of Kings. The key to David's achievement was his capture of Jerusalem and the transfer there of the ancient tribal rallying point, the Ark of the Covenant. By moving the Ark to Jerusalem, the new capital, David identified his regime with Israel's religion. Jerusalem, David's city, is the Holy City blessed by the presence of the Lord. When David's son Solomon built a magnificent Temple to house the Ark, the monarchy's role was reinforced: God in their midst was no longer the tent-dweller He had been with the tribes in the desert, but a King enthroned in His palace on Mount Zion, with the human king as His viceroy.

Now the covenant focused on the king, of whom God said: "You are my son; this day have I begotten you." [71] In token of the king's sacred character, he, like the Temple priests, was anointed with holy oil. Every king was the Lord's *mashiach* (Hebrew for

[71] Psalm 2:7.

"anointed one," anglicized as "messiah"). Through him, all the covenant blessings of peace and prosperity would come to the nation.[72]

The time of the monarchy was a Golden Age, but a short one. Through the ineptitude of Solomon's son, a fatal split took place in 928 B.C., resulting in two kingdoms: Israel in the north, composed of ten tribes, and Judah in the south, composed of the tribes of Judah and Benjamin plus the priestly tribe of Levi.[73] As was noted, neither kingdom was strong enough to withstand invasion from mighty enemies.

Worse, the people had strayed from God's will. They still believed in God, but contact with pagan religions led many Israelites to think of Him as a remote and impersonal power that had to be placated by ritual acts, that could in fact be almost controlled by a sort of magic expressed in the liturgy. If this ritual were meticulously carried out, they had done all that was asked of them and their "private" lives were no concern of God. So, side-by-side with divine worship flourished idolatry and social injustices.

Still, there were men who had an intuitive vision of God's order and the courage to express it fiercely. It was now that God spoke through these prophets to point the right way. There was Amos, for instance, the shepherd who condemned the luxury and flagrant injustice of the rich. And Hosea, who laid bare the heart of God and used the daring metaphor of the love of a husband for his own wife, even an unfaithful one. And Isaiah, who saw God's holiness like a consuming fire, and foretold the mysterious figure of the innocent sufferer whose self-oblation brings redemption to all.

Israel and Judah were wiped off the map, but God's people are still His: "As the shepherd rescues from the mouth of the lion two legs, or a piece of an ear,"[74] so God will spare a remnant to be the seed of a new growth. While exiled in Babylon from 587 to 539 B.C., the Jews learned that the obligations of the covenant were not confined to liturgy but involved personal commitment as well. God told them to "tear your hearts and not your garments."[75]

---

[72] See Psalm 71:1, 8–10, 16.
[73] 1 Kings 12:1–14:31.
[74] Amos 3:12.
[75] Joel 2:13.

Yahweh is a holy God who demands that His people, individually and collectively, "be holy, for I am holy."[76] Early in the Babylonian Captivity, Jeremiah prophesied a renewed covenant in which this principle will prevail: "The days are coming, says the Lord, when I will make a new covenant with the house of Israel and the house of Judah. . . . I will put my law within them, and I will write it upon their hearts; and I will be their God, and they shall be my people."[77] The God who had intervened in Israel's past, not once but many times, would intervene again.

Conversion, Conviction, Consummation

The time spent in Babylonian captivity was the watershed of Israel's history. We might say that the history of God's people as a nation ended and the history of Judaism began. For although the southern kingdom of Judah was gone, its religion, "Judaism," arose from the ashes as the prophets had foretold.

The nation was destroyed, said the prophets, for the simple reason that it had forsaken the covenant of Sinai, in virtue of which God was bound to defend Israel from all her enemies, provided Israel rendered proper tribute to God.[78] Under the wicked kings Manasseh and Amon (seventh century B.C.), Judah sank to astounding moral and spiritual depths.[79] The prophet Zephaniah, as recounted in the book bearing his name, sternly denounced the venal judges, the corrupt priests, the ruling classes who oppressed the poor, and the false prophets who gave favorable oracles in proportion to the pay they received. Society was rotten to the core.

As the exiled Judeans "sat by the rivers of Babylon and wept,"[80] they reasoned that Israel could hope to live again only by returning to the covenant. Led by their fellow-exile and prophet Ezekiel, they prayed, fasted, and openly confessed their own past offenses. False standards came down one by one. The cult of statism was demolished, the pride of the race humbled. No longer would they attribute their sufferings to the sins of

[76] Leviticus 11:45.
[77] Jeremiah 31:31–33.
[78] See Exodus 23:22.
[79] See 2 Kings 21; 2 Chronicles 33.
[80] Psalm 137:1.

their fathers, while using the latter's virtues as a screen for their own infidelities. "There shall no longer be anyone among you who will repeat this proverb in Israel: 'Fathers have eaten green grapes, thus their children's teeth are on edge.' . . . Only the one who sins shall die. . . . Why should you die, O house of Israel, . . . says the Lord God. Return and live." [81]

During this period all the sacred traditions of Israel, all the messages addressed to them by the prophets, most still handed down orally, were collected, edited, and copied by "Scribes." These Scriptures, it was realized, were not just national tradition but God's Word to them: it was revelation, which in turn called for faith.

So the People of God returned from Babylonia chastened, purified, and resolved henceforth to be God's covenant people. They had seen God's hand in their sufferings. Yahweh is a jealous God, and His people must bind themselves to Him only. Worship in the rebuilt Temple would take the place of battles to extend the kingdom: "In days to come, the mountain of the Lord's house shall be established. . . . All nations shall stream toward it; many peoples shall come and say: 'Come, let us climb the Lord's mountain.' . . . For from Zion shall go forth instruction, and the word of the Lord from Jerusalem." [82]

Faced with danger from hostile enemies and beset with temptations to despair, the Jews were sustained in their rekindled faith by new prophets: Haggai, Zachariah, and Malachi. Finally, Ezra and Nehemiah crowned the work begun in exile. On New Year's Day in 444 B.C., the people solemnly vowed "to walk in God's law which was given by Moses the servant of God." [83] This renewed dedication to the Mosaic Law cannot be stressed enough. All later institutions would rest on it: synagogues, schools, courts, rituals, and sects were established to preserve the true religion in the face of possible destruction from Greek, Syrian, and Roman invaders.

But such high ideals did not inspire the whole community, nor did they work a complete transformation. Some, for example, chafed at the humiliation of their national state. They longed for

[81] Ezekiel 18:2–4, 31–32.
[82] Isaiah 2:2–3.
[83] Nehemiah 10:29.

a great king, a new David, a messiah, who would lead the Jews to freedom and re-establish God's kingdom on earth. Others, the Pharisees, stressed the full observance of the Law to the minutest detail. Still others withdrew from the mainstream and went into the wilderness to share a common ascetical life while awaiting the final struggle between "the sons of light" (that is, themselves) and "the sons of darkness."

Underlying these assorted voices was a Word—intuited by pagan sages, spoken by God at Sinai, invoked by Israel's prophets. That Word was, in all its forms, God's own revelation of Himself, and God was now prepared to utter it in its final perfection.

"And the Word was made flesh and dwelt among us." [84] With these words, whatever truths we gleaned in Hinduism's god-man Krishna, Buddhism's selfless Bodhisattva, Confucianism's personal Heaven, Taoism's eternal Way, and Judaism's prophesied Savior find their fulfillment. The "desire of all nations" [85] and "hope of Israel" [86] became *Emmanuel*, "God with us" [87]—in Jewish flesh.

From Promise to Fulfillment

THE MESSIAH AS SON OF DAVID

"In many and various ways God spoke of old to our fathers by the prophets; but in these last days he has spoken to us by a Son...." [88] Judaism's knowledge of God, compared to the knowledge of the other religions we have explored thus far, is sunlight compared to fog. And yet God's final and complete utterance, so Christians contend, is His enfleshed Word, His Son. In Jesus of Nazareth, Divine Revelation reaches its unsurpassable fullness.

The Jewish Bible, or what Christians call the Old Testament, creates the climate of preparation, of longing for one who could give final meaning to God's plan in history. Of course, there is a big difference between preparation and fulfillment. The Old Testament opens perspectives and awakens hopes, but it tells a

[84] John 1:14.
[85] Haggai 2:7.
[86] Jeremiah 17:13.
[87] Isaiah 7:14.
[88] Hebrews 1:1–2.

story in need of a last chapter. Now, from the standpoint of Christian faith, we will begin to consider how Jesus not only fulfils what was promised, but gives the promises a new and deeper significance.

First, however, a caution. Christians will naturally want to highlight the individual Old Testament texts that give a kind of preview of Jesus. But these prophecies do not describe Him so clearly and unmistakably that one need only read the prophecies to find Christ fully present there. God gradually prepared Israel for the overwhelming reality of the Savior. At no stage of the preparation did any Jew adequately understand or even suspect the full meaning of the divine plan: that God Himself, the Second Person of the Trinity, would become man to die and rise for our salvation. Therefore, in the Christian's quest for neat mathematical equation between Old Testament prophecy and New Testament fulfillment, it is necessary to discern God's slow task of educating His people by couching the hope of the future in forms that would be meaningful for the present.

With that said, let us take up the question of the Messiah. Recall that the Hebrew word *mashiach*, "Messiah" (in Greek it is *Christos*, "Christ"), is used in the Old Testament to refer to those who received a ceremonial anointing with oil in the rite of assuming the offices of king and priest. Eventually the term came to be used in a technical sense to refer to Yahweh's anointed representative who would crush Israel's oppressors and usher in God's reign. Although the Messiah was assigned various powers and dignities, he was *not* thought of as divine. Salvation is the work of Yahweh alone, and Yahweh is free to save with or without the help of an anointed agent.

Because the title "Messiah" had political and nationalistic connotations, Jesus generally avoided using it of Himself, one exception being His conversation with the Samaritan woman in chapter 4 of the Gospel of John. Being a Samaritan and antagonistic toward Jews, she would be unlikely to interpret the term in the popular sense. Her people would be more inclined to view the Messiah as a universal savior, and many Samaritans did in fact come to acknowledge Jesus as "the Savior of the world." [89]

[89] John 4:42.

God had promised that the Messiah would be a descendant of King David, strong with the power of Yahweh, and would reign over a kingdom of justice and peace, perfectly fulfilling the ideal that had been imperfectly realized in David and his successors.[90]

The New Testament offers its own witness to the hope of a Davidic Messiah. Saint Joseph, the legal and putative father of Jesus, was a direct descendant of David,[91] and his legal paternity conferred rights of inheritance. It is less certain whether Mary, the virgin mother of Jesus, likewise came from the line of David, although Saint Paul hints at this in saying that Jesus was "descended from David according to the flesh,"[92] and certain Fathers of the Church maintained that Mary was of the house of David. Blind Bartimaeus addressed Jesus as "Son of David,"[93] as did the crowds who shouted their Hosannas as Jesus entered Jerusalem riding a donkey in accord with Zechariah's messianic prophecy.[94] A thousand years earlier, David's son Solomon rode a mule at his presentation as king to the cheering crowds of Jerusalem.[95] Jesus, on that first Palm Sunday, signified that He was the greater son of David.

It would overtax this study to describe all the perspectives the Old Testament opens up in its preparation for the Messiah. We can, however, look briefly at some other forms taken by Israel's messianic hope, besides the Davidic king. Becoming familiar with at least the main strands of "Messianism" will help us better appreciate the divinely directed longing and expectation that Christ answers.

THE MESSIAH AS SON OF MAN AND SUFFERING SERVANT

The messianic hope of the Jews expressed itself above all in the longing for a great king, a new David, who would save Israel from her enemies and inaugurate the reign of God. This form of Messianism took its rise from God's promise to David to give his

---

[90] For some key samplings of this royal messianic hope, read 2 Samuel 7:12–16, Isaiah 9:1–6, and Jeremiah 23:5–6.

[91] See the genealogy in Matthew 1:1–16.

[92] Romans 1:3.

[93] Mark 10:47.

[94] See Matthew 21:9, fulfilling Zechariah 9:9: "Behold, your king comes to you, triumphant and victorious is he, humble and riding on a donkey."

[95] See 1 Kings 1.

son an everlasting dynasty that would extend over all nations.[96] Thus, a royal descendant of David would fulfill God's promise to make Abraham the father of many.[97] Just as God raised up Moses to deliver Israel, the nation born of Abraham's son Isaac, from Egypt,[98] so it was for "my people Israel" that God established His covenant with David. This covenant between Yahweh and the house of David did not annul but rather absorbed the ancient Mosaic covenant between Israel and Yahweh.

It makes an interesting exercise to examine the historical record and count the number of those who were judged worthy of their great ancestor, David. Yet Yahweh would not go back on His word. Although the Babylonian exile and the return to Judah under Persian rule had put an end to kingship in Israel, the people never lost hope in a future ruler who would establish Yahweh's rule over the world. David's eternal kingship becomes, in the New Testament, the glorious reign of the risen Christ, Son of David through Saint Joseph.

But there are other strands of Messianism to consider. When Caiaphas asked Jesus, "Are you the Christ, the Son of the Blessed?" Jesus answered unequivocally, "I am," and immediately added that He, the Christ, would fulfill the glorious destiny of the "Son of Man."[99] The title "Son of Man," which Jesus preferred to use in speaking of Himself, had different meanings. It could signify human beings in general or, as in the mind of the prophet Daniel, an exalted heavenly figure who will appear in the end times.[100] Our Lord extended and enriched the Son of Man theme by associating it with His future Passion, Death, and Resurrection.[101] A humiliated and suffering Son of Man evokes another mysterious figure, namely, the Suffering Servant of Yahweh, as described in chapters 52 and 53 of the Book of Isaiah.

The fusion of these two themes, Son of Man and Suffering Servant, in the person of the Messiah is both novel and paradoxical. That this combination of ideas was hard to accept is shown

[96] See 2 Samuel 7:8–16.
[97] See Genesis 15:5–6; 17:4–8.
[98] See Exodus 2:23–25; 6:5.
[99] See Mark 14:60–62.
[100] See Daniel 7:13–14.
[101] As in Mark 8:31; 9:9; and 14:21.

by the reaction of the disciples, who were scandalized at the prospect of a dead Messiah. When we add to this new revelation Christ's prediction that His disciples would have to share His suffering, is it any wonder that they found this a hard teaching or that they were slow to grasp its profound significance? As Pope Benedict XVI remarks, "The scandal of the Cross is harder for many to bear than the thunder of Sinai had been for the Israelites."[102] Only the actual events themselves—Christ's Passion, Death and Resurrection, together with the sending of the Holy Spirit on Pentecost—would bring the light necessary to comprehend how the three main lines of messianic promise—Son of David, Son of Man, and Suffering Servant—were to be identified with Jesus of Nazareth.

Of course, not everyone came to believe in Jesus as the long-awaited Messiah of the Jews, never mind as God Incarnate. Ancient Jews and Christians eventually parted ways in their reading of Israel's Scriptures. For Christians, Jesus is the great new fact that guides a massive re-reading of the Old Testament. The Romans crucified Him as "King of the Jews," so that He might show Himself to be the messianic Son of David. Judaism condemned Him as a son of man, thus placing Him in the glorious light of the messianic fulfillment of the "Son of Man sitting at the right hand of Power and coming with the clouds of heaven."[103] And in the death of the Suffering Servant, who on Calvary gave His life as an offering for sin,[104] divine justice and mercy unite in humanly inconceivable fashion.

In what follows, we will consider other ways, besides these messianic themes, in which Jesus fulfills God's promises, including the promise that Israel is to be "a light to the nations."[105] We must also address the thorny question of Christianity's relation to Judaism and to the Jewish people, our "elder brothers in the faith of Abraham."[106]

---

[102] Benedict XVI, *Jesus of Nazareth: From the Baptism in the Jordan to the Transfiguration*, trans. Adrian J. Walker (New York: Doubleday, 2007), pp. 67–68.

[103] Mark 14:62.

[104] As prophesied in Isaiah 53:10.

[105] Isaiah 42:6.

[106] John Paul II, visit to the Great Synagogue of Rome, April 13, 1986.

A New and Eternal Covenant

The ancient covenant between God and Israel was crystallized in the Law given to Moses and expressed by God's dwelling with His people, first in the tabernacle of the desert, and later in the Jerusalem Temple. With Jesus Christ, a new covenant came into force. Christ is the anointed king, the messianic Son of David who, in a new "exodus," freed people from captivity to Satan, sin, and death by being "pierced for our offenses, crushed for our sins." [107] To the people gathered on the slopes of an open hillside He proclaimed: "Do not think that I have come to abolish the law and the prophets; I have come not to abolish them but to fulfill them." [108] Everything He said and did was always related to the first assertion that His work was a fulfillment of God's promises, especially since the days of Abraham.

It was no simple matter to see all that the Lord's work entailed. His closest disciples failed to comprehend the inner logic of His teaching. They witnessed His miracles and they heard His words, yet the two disciples of Emmaus probably spoke for all when they said regretfully, "But we had hoped that he was the one to redeem Israel." [109] They did not understand how a man, dying "accursed" on a cross, could be the long-awaited Messiah. And so, the risen Christ gave those puzzled followers a lesson in biblical interpretation, beginning with Moses and the prophets.

But of all the discussions Jesus had with some of the best minds in Judaism, His dialogue with Nicodemus the Pharisee perhaps captured His mission best. Jesus told Nicodemus, "Unless one is born of water and the Spirit, he cannot enter the kingdom of God." [110] He came not to destroy but to make all things new, and He was asking people to be reborn "from above." He could have cited God's promise to Israel—"A new heart I will give you, and a new spirit I will put within you . . ." [111] —but He had still greater truths for Nicodemus. In rapid order, He gave

[107] Isaiah 53:5.
[108] Matthew 5:17.
[109] Luke 24:21.
[110] John 3:5.
[111] Ezekiel 36:26.

insights into His heavenly origin, His future death, His testimony of God's love for all people, and the way of salvation that leads through faith in Him.[112]

The new spirit that Our Lord held out to Nicodemus was shown in His interpretation of the Law of Moses. External compliance with the letter of the Law is not enough, Jesus taught: the Law must be observed interiorly. This was the original ideal set before every child of the covenant: "Be holy, for I the Lord your God am holy." [113] To accomplish this there was required a new spiritual law written, not on stone tablets, but in human hearts. In six different sections of His "Sermon on the Mount," Jesus contrasted His interpretation of the Torah and the usual form of observance: "You have heard it said. . . . But I say to you . . ." [114] The Law of Moses prohibited homicide and adultery; Jesus forbade hatred and impure desires. The Law permitted a man to divorce his wife; Jesus commanded union until death. Far from making light of the Law, Jesus raised it to a dignity never before known.

Our Lord's work was crowned by His Death and Resurrection, but not before He had formed a new "People of God" into one body to bear His revelation to all nations. Thus, twelve Apostles assembled on Mount Zion in imitation of the twelve tribes of Israel on Mount Sinai. It was the traditional Passover meal, wherein all the wonders of God were commemorated and made to live again. Jesus proclaimed to them His new Law of loving others as He had loved them. He reviewed all the manifestations of God's love for Israel in bringing them forth from Egypt. Several times He referred to the "Kingdom of Heaven" and while doing so He gave them His Body and Blood under the appearances of bread and wine. "Do this in remembrance of me," [115] He instructed them, evoking the words of Yahweh at the first Passover: "This day shall be a memorial feast for you [...] a perpetual institution." [116]

The covenant constituting them the "New Israel" was established and sealed with Christ's Blood, shared at the Last Supper

---

[112] See John 3:10–21.
[113] Leviticus 19:2.
[114] Matthew 5:17–48.
[115] Luke 22:20.
[116] Exodus 12:14.

and shed on the Cross. Thus was fulfilled the new and eternal covenant prophesied in Jeremiah 31:31–33 and renewed in every celebration of the Eucharist. Christ is the true Temple wherein dwells God's glory. So too are the members of His body the Church: living stones joined to Christ the cornerstone, built up into God's dwelling place.[117]

To this new covenant people, Christ's holy Church, come also the blessings of the covenant: not now merely land and length of days but eternal life. And instead of a plot of land to call their national home, they have a *patria*, a true Fatherland in the heavenly City, the New Jerusalem that is to come. In the meantime, the Church offers no new and easy cures for the despair that warps so many lives. Her strength does not consist in ready-made solutions. Rather, faithful to the biblical tradition, she offers to the world the fulfilled hope of Israel.

A Story Still Unfolding

We have given the lion's share of our attention to Judaism, and with good reason: Christianity is inexplicable without Judaism. In this final section on Judaism, we take up a much vexed question: What is the present status of God's covenant with Israel?

Contrary to the expectations of the early Christians, Judaism did not come to an end after the destruction of Jerusalem and its Temple by the Romans in A.D. 70. Today, two thousand years after the coming of Christ, there exist Jewish communities that observe the ancient laws of Moses concerning the Sabbath, circumcision, diet, Passover, and so on. This fact raises questions to which Christians cannot be indifferent. Does the old covenant remain in force? That is to say, has God permanently willed the practice of Judaism?

The Catholic Church at the Second Vatican Council (1962–65) reiterated perennial Catholic teaching, based as it is on Scripture and the Church Fathers' reading of Scripture. Through Abraham and the other patriarchs, and after them through Moses and the prophets, God taught Israel "to acknowledge Him as the one

---

[117] See 1 Peter 2:4–5; Ephesians 2:20–22.

68

living and true God, provident Father and just Judge, and to wait for the Savior promised by Him, and in this manner prepared the way for the Gospel down through the centuries."[118] First, God "entered into a covenant with Abraham and, through Moses, with the people of Israel."[119] One and the same God "wisely arranged that the New Testament be hidden in the Old and that the Old be made manifest by the New."[120]

Christians, then, have a special bond with the Jews. However differently Jews and Christians may understand God's essence and actions, both profess faith in the one God of Abraham, Isaac, Jacob, and Jesus. The Church is conscious that she is a branch grafted onto the olive tree of Israel. On that basis she claims Abraham as her own patriarch or "father in faith."[121] The second-century priest Marcion was condemned as a heretic for teaching that the Christian Gospel had nothing to do with the Old Testament. Had he won the day, the Christian Bible would include only the New Testament—and even that trimmed by Marcion's scissors. Can any Christian read the prerogatives of Judaism enumerated in Saint Paul's Letter to the Romans without lowering his head in awe?[122]

Nevertheless, Judaism's role after Christ is limited. The New Testament, in certain passages, indicates that the old covenant has been replaced. Saint Paul contrasts the old covenant, carved on stone, which has lost its previous splendor, and the new covenant, written on human hearts by the Holy Spirit, which is permanent and burns brightly.[123] He speaks of Christ as "the end of the Law,"[124] apparently meaning its goal. The Mosaic Law yields to the "law of Christ"[125] or the "law of the Spirit."[126] Saint Thomas Aquinas, drawing on the Church Fathers and

---

[118] Second Vatican Council, Dogmatic Constitution on Divine Revelation *Dei Verbum*, no. 3.

[119] Ibid., no. 14.

[120] Ibid., no. 16.

[121] From the prayer *Supra quae* of the Roman Canon of the Mass.

[122] Romans 9:4–5: "They are the Israelites, and to them belong the sonship, the glory, the covenants, the giving of the law, the worship, and the promises; to them belong the patriarchs, and of their race, according to the flesh, is the Christ, who is God over all, blessed for ever. Amen."

[123] See 2 Corinthians 3:3.

[124] Romans 10:4.

[125] 1 Corinthians 9:21; Galatians 6:2.

[126] Romans 8:2.

medieval authorities, sought to reconcile these passages with Christ's assertion that He had come not to abolish but to fulfill the Law.[127] Aquinas distinguished the moral and ceremonial precepts of the old covenant: only the moral law (as expressed, above all, in the Commandments) endures, albeit in the fuller sense Christ gave it.

Fulfillment, then, is not abandonment. As the Apostle makes clear in Romans, chapters 9 through 11, the mysterious connection between the old and new covenants engages a still-unfolding story. The mystery of Israel and the mystery of the Church are mysteriously intertwined. Without any pretense of giving a definitive answer to the question at hand, it is possible to indicate some elements of a sound Catholic position.

While wanting to avoid Marcionism, we should not give the impression that there are two parallel covenants equally pleasing to God. As Cardinal Avery Dulles asserts: "Such a view is . . . irreconcilable with the New Testament and with the whole Catholic tradition. It is contrary to Vatican II (which expressed the hope that the whole world would recognize Jesus Christ as Savior), and incompatible likewise with current magisterial teaching, which is normative for Catholics."[128] At the same time, we should avoid arrogance when affirming Christianity as the fulfillment of Judaism. Just as the Exodus and Passover were fulfilled in Christian Baptism and the Eucharist, the sacraments of the new covenant are themselves fulfilled in Heaven.

We who confess Jesus as Christ and Lord should want to make Him known and loved by all, Jews included. To refuse to share with anyone the treasures that the Messiah brought to the world is a sin against charity. In the meantime, the old covenant is still in force in its most important aspect: God's gracious predilection for His Chosen People. "All Israel will be saved," the Apostle predicts.[129] Along the way to that fulfillment, Jews and Christians will dispute the most important question ever asked:

---

[127] See Matthew 5:17.

[128] "Avery Cardinal Dulles Replies," *First Things* 160 (February 2006): 6. Dulles was replying to a letter commenting on his essay "The Covenant with Israel," *First Things* 157 (November 2005): 16–21.

[129] Romans 11:26.

"Who do you say I am?"[130] And when it turns out that Christians have rightly named the Messiah all along, there will be no reason for boasting because then all glory will be to the God of Israel for His inclusion of us, all undeserving, in the drama of salvation.

Islam

Islam, which claims nearly 20 percent of the world's population, began in Arabia but is not primarily an Arabic religion. The country with most Muslims is Indonesia, followed by India. Turks are not Arabs, nor are Iranians, nor are the millions of Africans who are Muslims. Like Buddhism and Christianity, Islam has spread throughout the world, adapting itself culturally as it does so.

The Arabic word *Islam* means "submission" or "surrendering" and describes the attitude of the believer to God's will. Muslims do not speak of Muhammad as the founder of their religion so much as the final prophet of a truth that went back to Adam, was distorted over the years, and was recovered in its purity in the holy book of the Qur'an, which was revealed in stages to Muhammad over two decades. Muslims revere the Qur'an as the sacred word of God. For this reason, it cannot truly be translated. To be understood as God intends, it must be read in Arabic, the language in which it was revealed to Muhammad by the angel Gabriel.

Muhammad, the "seal of the prophets," was born around A.D. 570 in Mecca on the Arabian Peninsula. The desert was a place of wandering tribes and caravan trading centers. People worshiped nature spirits and honored numerous gods housed at a shrine in Mecca called Ka'ba. The orphaned Muhammad lived with an uncle, Abu Talib, working hard as a shepherd, camel driver, trader, and merchant. At the age of 25, he married a wealthy widow merchant fifteen years his senior, Khadija, with whom he had three daughters.

According to tradition, one night in the year 610, as Muhammad meditated on Mount Hira outside Mecca, he saw a vision

---

[130] Matthew 16:15

and heard a voice that demanded his obedience to the one God, Allah "Who teaches man that which he knew not." In insisting that Allah (the word means "God") was the only God and all others false, Muhammad angered those who profited from the worship of idols. He and his followers were ostracized by his tribe, being denied the ability to trade or associate with them. Persecution intensified after the deaths of Khadija and Abu Talib in 619. But while those in Mecca opposed Muhammad, tribal leaders in the city of Medina, about 200 miles to the north, sought his counsel. On July 16, 622, when a plot to assassinate Muhammad was discovered, Muhammad and his followers migrated to Medina, an event known as the *Hijra*, "migration." This date marks the beginning of the Muslim calendar.

Muhammad and his disciples rapidly became the most formidable political and military force in the region. The new religion was popular. It offered hope to the poor and disenfranchised as well as to the rich. Although it condoned polygamy in a land where men died young and women needed protection, it improved the treatment of women, recognizing their property rights and guaranteeing them equal footing with men in the afterlife.

The Qur'an urged propagation of the faith, so Muslims sought new converts by word and by sword. Expansion of Islam by war was considered a sacred duty, known as *jihad*. In 624, Muslims won a battle over their enemies at Badr and, after more bloody confrontations, finally managed to negotiate the peaceful surrender of Mecca in 630. Muhammad set an example of leniency for the vanquished that would continue in future Muslim campaigns and aid their success. Jews and Christians could keep their faith if they paid a tax, although they were frequently harassed.

Muhammad died in 632. During the decade between the Hijra and the prophet's death, Islam developed as a formal system. Muhammad's successors urged the faithful not to despair. Allah was almighty, they said. Muhammad was only a messenger, as had been Adam, Noah, Abraham, Moses, John the Baptist, and Jesus before him.

Jews and Christians are often surprised to learn how much of the biblical story is incorporated into Islam, and they are also surprised at the ways it is distorted in the process. In fact, Christians in the seventh and eighth centuries viewed Islam as a

Christian heresy rather than a new religion: this is how Saint John of Damascus (*ca.* 675–749), the first Christian theologian to give it serious attention, categorized it. Few today, however, dispute that Islam is a religion in its own right. Muslims profess reverence for Jesus and Mary but do not claim to be Christian. For them, as for Jews, the central Christian doctrines of the Trinity and the divinity of Jesus represent departures from Abraham's pure monotheism.

"There is no God but Allah and Muhammad is His prophet" is the complete Muslim creed. Both Judaism and Christianity adulterated the true faith by additions, subtractions, or distortions. The Qur'an is a "corrected" version of the Jewish and Christian Scriptures and presents the religion of Allah in its purity. Of course, Christians cannot accept this claim. They can, however, let it move them to a fresh appreciation of the "absurdity" of Christ, whose Incarnation has made the one only adorable God lovable.

Islam's Holy Book: The Qur'an

The arrangement of Islam's holy book, the Qur'an (Arabic for "recitation"), is an ancient convention. After the first *surah*, or chapter, which is an opening prayer, it is arranged in 113 surahs of decreasing length. Tradition says that Muhammad, who was barely literate, received the Qur'an as a series of revelations, dictated what he had heard, and was probably arranging the texts at the time of his death. Although the Qur'an is the center of Islamic faith, Muslims also revere the *hadiths*, the stories of Muhammad's life and sayings.

The Qur'an calls for complete submission to God's will. There is throughout a constant reminder of the rewards that await the righteous and the punishment that awaits evildoers. References to biblical figures are frequent. Abraham is the patriarch mentioned most often and commended for his absolute opposition to idolatry. Mary is upheld as a model of purity and obedience, and the virgin birth of Jesus is affirmed. However, Muslims deny that Jesus was crucified, for no true prophet could meet such an ignoble end. When Muslims speak of the prophets they mean especially Abraham, Isaac, Jacob, Moses, and Jesus, all of whom are seen as Muhammad's forerunners. In some verses of the Qur'an,

Jews and Christians are condemned, and Muslims are told never to befriend them. They will be punished for their refusal to accept Islam. Jews are seen as having betrayed the Torah, and Jesus' divinity is repeatedly denied. In other verses, Jews and Christians are portrayed as confused fellow "people of the Book," and the tone is more benign.

The Qur'an also contains dietary laws, punishments for specific crimes, as well as the obligations of believers toward their wives, children, debtors, orphans, and the poor. It emphasizes seeing everything in the light of God's will. Although women are clearly regarded in it as inferior to men, in its historical context the Qur'an was an advance: women have rights and are to be treated justly; polygamy is permitted only if a man can provide for all his wives and children; and there are repeated condemnations of what was at the time (seventh century) the common practice of female infanticide.

As was noted, Muslims believe that Jews and Christians were given God's truth, but that their Scriptures became corrupted with errors. Their quarrels, both with each other and within their own traditions, are cited as proof of their confusion. The Qur'an, Muslims believe, is the unadulterated Word of God as it came to Muhammad verbatim from Allah through the archangel Gabriel. One of Islam's most prominent contemporary scholars, Seyyed Hossein Nasr, writes:

> The text of the Quran is thus not based on long periods of compilation and interpretation by human agents. Rather, the Quran is the actual Word of God as revealed to His Messenger and is like Christ for Christians, who is himself the Word of God brought into the world through the Virgin Mary. She, therefore, plays a role analogous to that of the soul of the Prophet; both are pure, immaculate, and virginal before the Divine Word.[131]

Nasr goes on to say that the chanting of the Qur'an can cause spiritual rapture even in a person who knows no Arabic. The sacredness of the text is mysteriously transmitted across the barrier of human language and is felt by those hundreds of millions

---

[131] Seyyed Hossein Nasr, ed., *Islamic Spirituality*, vol. 1: *Foundations* (New York: Crossroad, 1987), p. 4.

of non-Arab Muslims, whose hearts palpitate in the love of God and whose eyes are moistened by the tears of joy upon simply hearing the Qur'an chanted.

In a different context, Nasr's remarks could inspire a rethinking of prejudices against traditional forms of Catholic worship. First, just as the proclamation of the Qur'an captivates body and soul before it appeals to the mind, so the Church's liturgy is not about understanding every spoken word but about worship, which is a whole-body, whole-person experience. When the purpose of the Sacred Liturgy comes to be seen *primarily* as a means of instruction or moral exhortation, such that ritualized gestures, silence, incense, bells, and other nonverbal symbols are neglected, poorly catechized Catholics flock elsewhere, often to Eastern religions or New Age, for a chance to experience a mystery beyond the ordinary.

Second, just as the chanted Arabic of the Qur'an stirs the hearts of Muslims of all languages, so Gregorian Chant—the "supreme model for sacred music" [132] and the musical form "specially suited to the Roman liturgy" [133] —captivates millions, Catholic and non-Catholic alike, who speak no Latin. The listener immediately perceives it as beyond ordinary emotion, timeless and sublime.

Third, just as Arabic unites the worldwide Muslim community in prayer, so Latin, the official language of the Catholic Church in the West, can link (and for many centuries *has* linked) local congregations to the universal Church extended through space and time. Indeed, nearly every major religion employs a special language for worship, thus underscoring the uniqueness of what is being celebrated while transcending borders, cultures, and ages. And universality is a big part of what "catholic" means.

The Five Pillars of Islam

The most important Muslim practices are the Five Pillars of Islam: the profession of faith (*Shahadah*), ritual prayer (*salat*),

---

[132] Pius X, Motu Proprio on Sacred Music *Tra le sollecitudini* (November 22, 1903), no. 3.
[133] Second Vatican Council, Constitution on the Sacred Liturgy, *Sacrosanctum Concilium*, no. 116.

almsgiving (*zakat*), fasting (*sawm*), and pilgrimage to Mecca (*Hajj*).

Shahadah is in a sense Islam's creed: "There is no God but Allah and Muhammad is His Prophet." This is obviously a rejection of polytheism. It is likewise an affirmation of God's sovereignty and of Muhammad's role as the final revealer of God's word in a line that includes Adam, Abraham, Moses, and Jesus.

Salat consists of silent and spoken prayers, bows, and prostrations, to be performed five times a day: at dawn, noon, the middle of the afternoon, sunset, and night. Vocal prayers are to be recited in Arabic. Salat should be done in the state of ritual purity, normally after an ablution or washing, and facing in the direction of the holy city Mecca. Ideally, the prayers are said with other Muslims in a mosque, but they may be done privately on any clean ground or on a rug. Muslims say these prayers in the name of all mankind—in fact, of all creation.

Zakat requires that a portion of one's income be given to charity, to the relief of the poor (either directly or to the Islamic state that supports the poor from these alms), or to the freeing of slaves and prisoners. The Qur'an frequently speaks of the importance of charity and says, for example, that debtors should be given ample time to repay, although it is much better simply to forgive the debt.

Sawm is obligatory for adults during the ninth lunar month, Ramadan, when Muslims commemorate the 23 years during which the Qur'an was revealed to Muhammad. Eating, drinking, smoking, and sexual activity are forbidden from dawn to sunset. The fast, which ends with a feast on the first day of the tenth month, is intended to promote self-discipline, make prayer easier, and deepen one's sympathy for the poor.

Every able-bodied Muslim who can afford it is expected to make a pilgrimage to Mecca at least once. The *Hajj* involves a visit to the Grand Mosque and a walk seven times around the Ka'ba ("cube"), an ancient granite structure. According to the Qur'an, the Ka'ba was built by Adam and restored by Abraham and his son Ishmael as a house of monotheistic worship. By the time of Muhammad, however, it had been taken over by pagan Arabs to house their many tribal gods. When Muhammad conquered Mecca in A.D. 630, he destroyed the idols inside the Ka'ba and rededicated it to the one true God. Thus, pilgrims who visit the Ka'ba get in touch with the pure state of religion that had existed before the fall of Adam. To remove distinctions of wealth and status during the Hajj, all men dress identically: two sheets of plain white, unhemmed cotton; women may wear any modest clothing. Before performing the Hajj, Muslims are recommended to discharge all debts and seek the forgiveness of anyone they have offended.

Some might consider jihad, or holy war, a virtual sixth pillar of Islam. There is, however, much controversy within Islamic society over what constitutes a jihad. The general Muslim interpretation of jihad is restricted to war waged in defense of Islamic religion and society, or, more broadly, any spiritual striving to live according to God's will. Yet there are Muslim extremist groups that consider Western society as a whole a mortal enemy of Islam, and so they legitimize terrorism as self-defense against a culturally decadent West. Although we should not allow our consideration of Islam to be dominated by much that is today done in the name of Islam, we do well to recall that the early Christians attracted pagans to join them because they excelled in virtue and mutual affection. They did not practice divorce, adultery, infanticide, or abortion. It is a great scandal that so many Christians of our day, while continuing to be identified as members of the Church, neglect their baptismal call to holiness.

Professions of faith, ritual prayer, almsgiving, fasting (followed by feasting), pilgrimages, and holy wars all have their place in Judeo-Christian tradition, as well. Some of the parallels are especially intriguing.

Muslims pray five times a day. Millions of Christians—laity, Religious, and clergy—sanctify the day by praying at set times the Liturgy of the Hours, which consists of five major parts: the Office of Readings, Morning Prayer or Lauds, Daytime Prayer (divided into the "little hours" of Terce, Sext and None), Evening Prayer or Vespers, and Night Prayer or Compline.

Muslims pray in the direction of Mecca. In the early Church there was no disagreement about the importance of churches, along with clergy and people, facing east in prayer, toward the coming Lord symbolized by the rising sun.

Muslims pray in the name of all creation. Saint Maximus the Confessor (580–662) taught that man, being composed of matter and spirit, is a microcosm of the universe and therefore a "priest of creation," standing between earth and Heaven. Christ, the "last Adam"[134] brought together or "recapitulated" in Himself all that has ever been, reconciling everything with God.[135] It is in the Eucharist, above all, that humanity and with it the whole of creation is sanctified: the Church, the community of men and women divinized in Christ through the Holy Spirit, offers bread and wine to the Creator, and receives them back changed into the very God to whom they were offered. Thus, an Islamic intuition informed by the biblical view of man as the pinnacle of creation is fulfilled beyond all imaginings in the Body of Christ: Church and Eucharist are the *axis mundi*, the center of all that is.

The Varieties of Islam

After Muhammad's death in A.D. 632, the Islamic community split into two major groups. One was led by Muhammad's cousin and son-in-law, Ali, who claimed appointment by the Prophet himself. The larger and politically more successful party chose Abu Bakr, Muhammad's closest friend and one of the early converts to Islam. These successors of Muhammad were called caliphs, or deputies. They were to rule Islam and the Islamic Arab state as Muhammad did, but they claimed no prophetic role, for all agreed that prophecy died with Muhammad.

The Ali faction became known as the Shi'ite Muslims (from *shiat-Ali*, "partisans of Ali"), while the majority following Abu Bakr became known as the "people of the sunna" (*sunna* means custom or tradition) or Sunni Muslims. Whereas the Sunnis believed that the caliphs elected to succeed Muhammad were Islam's legitimate authorities, the Shi'ites insisted that only the descendents of Ali, or imams, could rule. The Shi'ites were the eventual losers in a violent, decades-long struggle for mastery, a fact now reflected by their minority status within global Islam. Today 85 percent of all Muslims are Sunnis; the remaining 15 percent, mostly Iranians and Iraqis, are Shi'ites. According to Shi'ite tradition, the twelfth Imam, al-Mahdi (ninth century), was taken up into the supernatural realm and will return before the

---

[134] 1 Corinthians 15:45.
[135] See Ephesians 1:10.

end of the world as champion of the faithful (much as Christians hold that the risen Jesus ascended to Heaven and will return); in the meantime, the religious governors of the community are the ayatollahs, a title of recent origin and unknown to classical Islamic history.

Then there is Sufism, commonly described as Islam's esoteric or mystical dimension. Its name derives from *suf*, a word meaning wool, and was originally applied to those Muslim ascetics who, in imitation of Christian hermits, clad themselves in coarse woolen garb as a sign of penitence and renunciation of worldly vanities. Sufism has had a great influence in many parts of the Islamic world as well as among Western artists and intellectuals—although, in the West, mysticism in general has taken on a peculiarly New Age flavor and has occasioned a good deal of pop-culture flimflam. All Muslims are obliged to practice *shari'a*, Islamic morality and law. But Sufis, besides keeping the Five Pillars of Islam, seek an authentic, personal experience of God through a spiritual interpretation of the Qur'an aimed at finding its underlying meaning, and by the disciplines of asceticism, repetition of God's names, meditation, and trance.

Many Muslims regard Sufism as heretical because, in their view, the idea of intimate, loving union with God compromises God's absolute otherness, just as the Christian doctrines of the Trinity and the Incarnation are understood as false teachings that threaten pure monotheism. Jews, Christians, and Muslims all agree that there is an infinite difference between creature and Creator, to whom the creature's very existence is owed. Mainstream Islam's appraisal of Sufism is only made dimmer by Sufis who claim exemption from prayer and fasting. However, the vast majority of Sufis faithfully observe shari'a and acknowledge that closeness to God is a sheer gift.

Sufism, its adherents insist, has been present in Islam from the start: Muhammad himself being the first Sufi and the Qur'an providing Sufism's doctrinal basis. Surah 50:16, for instance, declares that God is "nearer to [man] than his jugular vein," and surah 73:20 calls God "the best and most beautiful recompense."

According to a *hadith,* or saying attributed to the Prophet, Muhammad identified three stages of spiritual development: the first is *al-islam*, voluntary submission to shari'a; the second is *al-iman*, faith, when grace enters the soul and the Muslim begins to love God's laws; and the third is *al-ihsan*, perfect virtue, the state of complete freedom from worldly attachments and absolute commitment to God's will. This classification is almost certainly one of many examples of direct Christian influence on Islam. Beginning with Origen in the third century A.D., the Christian mystical tradition likewise sets forth three stages of the spiritual life and describes them in similar terms: first, the *purgative*, in which the soul strives to give up sin; second, the *illuminative*, in which the soul applies all its energies to advancing in virtue; and finally, the *unitive*, in which the soul rests in God, generously resigned to the Divine Will.

Recall the same emphasis on humility and self-transcendence in the great religious traditions of the East, Hinduism and Buddhism. In their mature form, all religions tell us that one must get rid of the false ego, the inflated self-importance, in order to open up to the presence of the Divine. Some modern Sufi teachers have, in fact, downplayed Sufism's Islamic origin, presenting it as an eternal wisdom that resides in all mystical traditions. We might call it a "seed of the Word," the full significance of which emerges in Christian faith and life. For the Gospel likewise teaches that ultimate fulfillment will be found not in self-sufficiency but in self-emptying. More astonishingly, it begins with a self-emptying love originating outside ourselves, transfiguring everything, and alone able to raise us not only to the heights of divinity but, better still, to partake of God's own Life.

Islam and the Gospel

We are ready now to examine Islam in the light of Christian faith. Islam has a powerful sense of God's transcendence: His greatness, His majesty, His incomparability with anything else. It rejects the Christian doctrine of the Trinity, reasoning that the one God and Creator of all neither begets nor is begotten. "How can Allah have a son when he has no consort?" asks the Qur'an,[136] as if the divine Fatherhood and Sonship within the Trinity were a

[136] Qur'an 6:101.

matter of biology. It warns the people of the Book (Jews and Christians) to "believe in Allah and His messengers, and say not 'Three.' . . . Allah is only one God,"[137] and it denounces Trinitarianism as blasphemy.[138] These Qur'anic passages indicate a profound misunderstanding of the God whom Christians name Father, Son, and Holy Spirit.

Possibly the Qur'an was responding to something other than the orthodox Christian doctrine of the Trinity—the terminology of "three Persons in God" is, to say the least, easily misleading—though Muslims would take offense at this suggestion, as it implies that Muhammad, rather than God, was the author of the Qur'an, or else that God misunderstood Christian teaching. It is a difficult challenge to convince Muslims (and Jews) that the doctrine of the Trinity, rather than contradicting God's oneness, reveals the full dimensions of that perfect Unity. Here we plunge into the rich depths of Christian theology.

In the language of the Nicene-Constantinopolitan Creed, the Son is "eternally begotten of the Father," not as a creature but as "Light from Light, true God from true God." There was never a time when the Son did not exist, because His innermost being or essence is the same as that of the Father (and the Holy Spirit). Father, Son, and Spirit are each equally and fully God, without beginning or end. What distinguishes each Divine Person is precisely His relation to the other two. The Father *is* the very act of paternity by which He begets the Son in the perfect love of the Spirit. The Son *is* the very act of sonship by which He is eternally generated by the Father in the same perfect love of the Spirit. The Holy Spirit *is* the very act by which the Father and Son perfectly love each other. God the Holy Trinity is a movement of mutual giving and receiving of love. This is what the Bible means when it declares, "God is love."[139]

This is heady stuff. But it helps explain why we human beings, created as we are in the divine image, feel more whole, more "at one" with ourselves when we lose ourselves in love of another. Our relations are at the core of who we are because relations are at the core of who God is. When it comes to God and His image

[137] Qur'an 4:171.
[138] Qur'an 5:73.
[139] 1 John 4:8.

in human beings, plurality and unity are mutually supportive, like Taoism's yin/yang.

A necessary part of being Christian is believing that God in His Second Person became human: the man Jesus Christ. Likewise, a necessary part of being Muslim is denying the Incarnation. Islam denies the divinity of Christ for the same reason it denies the Trinity, namely, to defend the notion of *tawhid*, the absolute oneness of God. Allah does not sire offspring—not in the dim mist of eternity, and certainly not in the realm of time and matter.

What, then, does Islam teach about Jesus? The Qur'an calls Jesus (*Isa*, in Arabic) "God's messenger and Word" [140] but denies His divinity in the same verse and elsewhere. It teaches that Jesus was one of only two men (the other being Adam) who were immediately created by God rather than having a human father. [141] It acknowledges His virgin birth from Mary after the message of an angel. [142] It reports miracles worked by Jesus by God's permission, including some not found in the four canonical Gospels. [143]

Nevertheless, the Jesus of the Qur'an is very unlike the Jesus of the New Testament. He is not the eternal Son of God and Savior of the world. There is no divine Incarnation; no atoning Sacrifice for the sins of the world; no Resurrection, Ascension and present reign. At one point the Qur'an actually denies that Jesus' enemies killed Him, saying, "it only seemed so to them." [144] According to Muslim tradition, Judas Iscariot was miraculously made to look like Jesus and was crucified in His place while Jesus was secretly taken up to God. [145] While most Muslims believe Jesus will return to earth at the end of time, it will not be to judge the living and the dead and to establish His Kingdom; rather, He will proclaim Islam and usher in an age of unprecedented prosperity.

[140] Qur'an 4:171.

[141] See Qur'an 3:59.

[142] See Qur'an 3:42–47.

[143] See Qur'an 3:49; 5:110.

[144] Qur'an 4:157.

[145] This tradition owes much to the so-called Gospel of Barnabas, which even Muslim scholars acknowledge to be a medieval forgery written to curry favor with Muslims of the time.

The differences between Islam and Christianity concerning the fundamental human problem and its solution flow from their fundamental disagreements about God and Jesus Christ. Christianity teaches that human beings are born into sin as a consequence of Adam's fall from grace,[146] with rebirth in Christ as the only way of salvation.[147] The story of the Fall in Genesis 3 is told also in the Qur'an,[148] but with key differences: it did not break the human relationship with God; it did not result in death (which is part of the natural human lot); and its effect was not passed on to anyone else, except as a bad example. Thus, Islam teaches original human frailty calling for divine guidance, not original sin calling for a Redeemer. From this it follows that the ultimate aim that Islam commends is but a pale reflection of salvation in the Christian sense.

For Christians, the term "salvation" has various shades of meaning. Western Christianity typically describes salvation as deliverance from sin, death, and demonic powers, whereas the Christian East prefers to speak of deification (literally, "being made God") by the indwelling of the Holy Spirit. Either way, the underlying reality is the same: ultimate communion with the Trinity and, on that basis, with all the saved.

The Qur'an presents salvation as escape from the punishment of hellfire to the joy of Paradise.[149] In Paradise there are rivers of water, wine, and honey; springs and fountains with pebbles of precious stones; "pure consorts," created in perfection, with whom carnal joys are shared; but the supreme delight is acceptance by Allah.[150] As an aside, we Christians may scoff at such sensual imagery, but it behooves us to ponder whether we have been too shy in describing what the Lord has in store. For what purpose, after all, did Saint John record his visions of the heavenly Jerusalem, complete with golden streets, pearly columns, and jeweled walls? [151] The "new heaven and new earth" is *this* heaven and *this* earth transfigured in eternity. As theologian Robert Jenson explains: "Because Jesus lives to triumph, there will be the

---

[146] See Romans 5:12–21.
[147] See John 3:3.
[148] See Qur'an 2:29–39; 7:11–26; 15:26–40; and 20:15–24.
[149] Qur'an 3:185, for example.
[150] See Qur'an 9:27.
[151] See Revelation 21:1–27.

real Community, with its real Banquet in its real City amid its real Splendor, as no penultimate community or banquet or city or splendor is really just and loving or tasty or civilized or golden." [152]

What stands in the way of salvation for Muslim and Christian alike is the fact that God justly punishes sins. The Qur'an states that everyone goes to Hell and that, after some time, Allah will deliver some as He chooses. Only those who die in *jihad* gain Paradise immediately.[153] In Christian revelation, on the other hand, Hell is the fate of the damned only. Moreover, the doctrine of the eternity of Hell has been firmly in place since at least the seventh century and is a matter of Catholic faith.

The Muslim pursues salvation through the Five Pillars of Islam, believing that he will be rewarded in proportion to his good deeds, his restraint from evil deeds, and his faith. As long as there is life, there is hope for salvation, for Allah forgives sins.[154] Christianity teaches that God desires the salvation of all [155] and that salvation comes from the redeeming grace of Christ, who "was put to death for our trespasses and raised for our justification." [156] The New Testament confidently proclaims the saving power of faith in Jesus as Lord. Catholics and Protestants disagree as to whether one is saved through faith *alone* or through faith enlivened by charity and fruitful in good works. Together, however, they affirm that salvation is not earned through any deeds or merits of our own. Salvation is entirely God's gift, conferred through the Father's sheer graciousness, out of the love He bears us in His Son. "By grace you have been saved through faith; and this is not your own doing, it is the gift of God." [157] By faith we repent of our sins and adhere freely to the Gospel, knowing that "there is no condemnation for those who are in Christ Jesus." [158]

By preserving the monotheistic faith of Abraham, Islam was a great step forward in the religious and cultural developments of

---

[152] Robert W. Jenson, "How the World Lost Its Story," *First Things* 36 (October 1993): 19–24 at p. 23. Reprinted in *First Things* 201 (March 2010): 31–37.

[153] See Qur'an 19:67–68, 71–72.

[154] Qur'an 4:48 and 39:53 (among others).

[155] See 1 Timothy 2:4.

[156] Romans 4:25.

[157] Ephesians 2:8.

[158] Romans 8:1.

Arabs, Turks, Persians, and other formerly pagan peoples. Yet, in upholding Allah as the one God, Islam could accept Christ only as a prophet. From a Christian perspective, much more has been lost than gained by this. Blessed John Paul II expressed respect for the "religiosity of Muslims" and their "fidelity to prayer." [159] Muslims, he suggested, may be a powerful witness to Christians who have lost a sense of humility before God. But the Pope went on to say: "In Islam, all the richness of God's self-revelation, which constitutes the heritage of the Old and New Testaments, has definitely been set aside." [160] Putting it bluntly: Islam truncates the truth of God. Allah "is ultimately a God outside of the world, a God who is *only Majesty, never Emmanuel,* God-with-us." [161]

If Islam has a providential role, it is that of witnessing to the divine unity and challenging any notions that would deny or diminish that oneness. At the same time, the Church proclaims the good news that God's unity is not closed to us but open to us. Through the Sacred Humanity of Christ, present especially in the sacraments, Christians are drawn into the unifying and life-giving communion of the one true God who is Father, Son, and Holy Spirit.

Junior Monotheisms: Baha'i and Sikhism

Two other religions in the monotheistic tradition, both relatively small and young, are worthy of mention here: Baha'i and Sikhism.

Baha'i grew out of the Shi'ite branch of Islam. In the 1840s, a young Iranian scholar who called himself The Bab ("Gate") preached that a messenger would soon arrive from God, who would be the latest in a line of prophets including Moses, Krishna, Buddha, Jesus, and Muhammad. Because this teaching contradicted Islam's belief that Muhammad was God's final prophet, the Bab and his disciples faced instant persecution and, in 1850, The Bab was executed. After a struggle for succession

---

[159] John Paul II, *Crossing the Threshold of Hope*, ed. Vittorio Messori, trans. Jenny McPhee and Martha McPhee (New York: Alfred A. Knopf, 1994), p. 93.

[160] Ibid., p. 92.

[161] Ibid., emphasis in original.

and years of exile, Mirza Husayn Ali Nuri, a leader in the Baghdad community of Babists, proclaimed himself, in 1863, to be the prophet foretold by The Bab. He called himself Baha'ullah, "the glory of God." Such was his influence that the Ottoman authorities exiled him and many of his followers to Palestine (now Israel) where he was imprisoned for nine years in the fortress of Acre. Shortly after his release, the founder of Baha'i went to live near Haifa, where he remained until his death in 1892.

Within a year or two, Westerners began to show an interest in the new religion, and during the first years of the twentieth century, small groups of Baha'is could be found in Europe and America. Most Baha'is today are converts from non-Islamic backgrounds. Baha'is emphasize the unity of humanity, equal rights for men and women, monogamy, compulsory education, and a just social order. Their worship is informal and usually takes place in private homes or rented spaces. Prayers and devotional texts are read, and food and drink shared. Prayer is offered every day, but instead of facing the Muslim holy city of Mecca, Baha'is face the direction of Baha'ullah's tomb in Acre. Pilgrimage, usually to Baha'i shrines in Israel, is also stressed. There is an annual period of fasting. Other observances include naming ceremonies for babies, marriage, and funerals.

Baha'i has a worldwide membership estimated at four million, but it is making new converts in India, Africa, Latin America, and among Pacific islanders. The largest concentration of members is still found in Iran, where the faith is routinely persecuted because of its deviation from Islam and its ties to Israel.

We turn now to Sikhism, which takes its name from the Punjabi word for "student" or "seeker of truth." A hybrid of Hinduism and Islam, Sikhism originated in the Punjab region of northwest India at a time when most of India was under Muslim rule. Despite its Indian origin, Sikhism was not among the Asian religions treated earlier in this book, on account of its strict monotheism (owing largely to Muslim influence). While some Sikh beliefs bear the marks of the shared Hindu and Muslim past, Sikhism is unique. Since 80 percent of Sikhs live in Punjab, Sikhism may not seem a world religion; yet North America and Great Britain have growing Sikh populations. Sikh men are recognized by their turbans, uncut hair (contained in the turbans), beards, ceremonial daggers, and steel wristbands.

The founder of Sikhism, Guru Nanak, was born into a Hindu family in 1469 at Talwandi in present-day Pakistan. At age thirty, Nanak went to the river as usual one day to make his morning prayers. After a disappearance of three days, during which he was presumed drowned, Nanak returned home and, after a day of silence, made his famous utterance: "God is neither Hindu nor Muslim, and the path I follow is God's."

Guru Nanak died in 1539 and was succeeded by nine other gurus, of whom the last died in 1708. Whereas in Hinduism any spiritual guide may be called a guru, in Sikhism the word is used only of God Himself, the ten gurus, and the Sikh holy scriptures, known as the Adi Granth ("original book") or, more honorifically, the Guru Granth Sahib ("the honorable guru in book form"). The Adi Granth consists of the writings of six gurus, expressed in metric verse, in addition to verses from the Hindu and Muslim traditions. God is the true Guru; Nanak and the nine others who also have the title, as well as the Adi Granth, are called guru because they express divine truth.

Initiates into Sikhism drink *amrit*, sugared water that has been stirred with a double-edged sword. Sikh worship takes place in a *gurdwara* ("gateway to the guru"), the key area of which is a spacious room housing the Adi Granth. This building is also used as a center for social activity and has a community kitchen attached to it. Like Hindus, Sikhs believe in the cycle of birth, death, and rebirth, from which the only way out is to achieve liberation from the binding effect of karma. But unlike Hinduism's four possible paths to enlightenment, liberation in Sikhism is attained only through God's grace.

The whole of Sikh theology is encapsulated in the *Mulmantar* ("root formula"), the opening section of the Adi Granth. Composed by Guru Nanak and recited by Sikhs every morning, it professes: "There is one Supreme Being, the Eternal Reality, the Creator, without fear and devoid of enmity, immortal, beyond birth and death, self-existent, known by the Guru's grace."

IV

CHRISTIANITY

IT is useful to review briefly the ground we have covered. Although the idea of a creator God is not at the center of the religious traditions of India and the Far East, and in some cases not even part of the picture, we have discovered in Eastern religion glimpses and intuitions of the God who reveals Himself even as He conceals Himself. Within the biblical orbit we found additional knowledge of God (for those who accept it) in direct revelations to particular human beings in historical time: Adam and Eve, Abraham, Moses, and the prophets of Israel. We reviewed the highlights of the centuries-long drama of the religious journey of the children of Israel, as it is recorded in the Old Testament, and were brought to a deeper appreciation of the Jewish origins of Christianity.

From there we turned to Islam, a derivative of Judaism and Christianity. In spite of Islam's absolute monotheism and other doctrines it has in common with Judaism and Christianity, neither Jews nor Christians can accept Muhammad as a prophet. It is hard to recognize the God of the Bible in the God of the Qur'an, and two very different concepts of the human person have emerged from the Christian and Muslim understandings of God. Lastly we took note of Baha'i, a heretical offshoot of Islam, and Sikhism, a monotheistic religion blending elements of Islam and Hinduism.

Taking all of this into account, it seems that it is only with Jews that Christians can know for certain that they pray to the same God—the God of Abraham, Isaac, Jacob, and Jesus. Although Christians profess the one God of Israel in three distinct Persons, it is undoubtedly the God of Israel whom they profess. Moreover, they profess Him as a Trinity according to His final revelation in Jesus of Nazareth, the Jew who fulfills the hope of Israel and is Savior of the world.

We now stand at the threshold of the Church, the communion of faith and charity, the community of saints who are Christ's own very members as His Body and Bride. In what follows, we will traverse the various Christian communities outside the Catholic fold, beginning with those that separated themselves from the Catholic unity in the first Christian millennium and have survived to this day. Next we will look at the Orthodox Churches of the East, which definitively broke communion with the Catholic Church in 1054 but which are very close to Catholicism in terms of apostolic doctrine, sacramental worship, and ordered ministry. Then we shall explore the various forms of Protestantism, some of which are more in contact with their Catholic roots than others.

The divisions among Christians, while sad and scandalous, are at times unavoidable. Truth obliges, and sometimes truth divides. There are different and sometimes conflicting ways of understanding and adhering to "the faith once for all delivered to the saints." [162] The Catholic Church has a very definite position on what constitutes Christian orthodoxy, a position for which it claims the authority of two thousand years of doctrine, institutionalized in the Church's *Magisterium* or teaching office. Our chief interest is to recognize the ways in which Catholicism complements and enriches the authentically Christian elements present in those separated churches and communities. Having done that, we will better appreciate what the English Catholic apologist Cecily Hastings had in mind when she wrote: "Whenever there is a choice between giving to some part of the Christian revelation either a more expansive, many-dimensioned, richly complex, open interpretation or, alternatively, a narrower, flatter, thinner, more restricted one, the former is always the Catholic one." [163]

The Parameters of Christian Orthodoxy

God willed to reveal Himself and to enter into an intimate personal relation with mankind. This revelation and plan of salva-

[162] Jude 3.
[163] Cecily Hastings, untitled essay in *Born Catholics*, ed. F. J. Sheed (New York: Sheed & Ward, 1954), p. 170.

tion began to unfold through Moses and the prophets, but only in Christ do we find the fulfillment. He is the Incarnate Word of God, the embodiment of all God wants us to know about Himself. Revelation, then, is the total message of God as given in and through His Son.

Christ established a Church to bear witness to this saving message until the end of time.[164] The Apostles who experienced Christ and His message firsthand are the foundation stones of this Church. We would be mistaken, however, to imagine that their knowledge of God's revelation in Christ was all thought out and formulated into precise language. What they communicated to the Church was not a catechism but the totality of the Good News in terms of a lived experience. This message is called the "Deposit of Faith." [165]

Anything not already contained in the Deposit of Faith can never be proclaimed as part of the Christian Faith. However, the Church in every age receives the Deposit of Faith partly as things known explicitly, and partly as a lived experience that has yet to be reflected upon and articulated. The implications of a particular doctrine can gradually become clearer, thus making it possible, even necessary, for that doctrine to be refined and amplified. Developments of doctrine are legitimate, provided they are consistent with the truths from which they originate. This idea of continuity in Divine Revelation is summed up in one word: Tradition—from the Latin noun *traditio*, something handed on.

Tradition is enshrined in the books of the Bible. The Old Testament is the story of God's breaking into history, choosing a people, and entering into covenant with them—one collective, great event to be remembered and transmitted both orally and in writings, sometimes by borrowed imagery (serpent, flood), sometimes by portrayal of God as shepherd or husband, but especially in the liturgy of Israel's worship. This lived Tradition, which made God's revelation alive to each succeeding generation, surged onward to its full realization in Christ. The New Testament recounts the earliest Christians' experience of Christ. Formulated within the Church, these writings were gradually

[164] See Matthew 28:18–20.
[165] See 1 Timothy 6:20; 2 Timothy 1:13–14.

recognized as divinely inspired. The Bible, then, is a fruit of Tradition and exists within Tradition.

Because the infinite richness of revelation unfolds in time, Tradition encompasses not only Scripture but also the doctrinal definitions following from new insights into God's revealed Word. Many Christian doctrines were formulated at general or "ecumenical" councils, gatherings of all the bishops of the world presided over by the pope. There have been 21 ecumenical councils in the history of the Catholic Church, from Nicaea I (325) to Vatican II (1962–1965). The earliest councils solidified the preeminence of the five principal Christian dioceses, called "patriarchates"—Rome, Alexandria, Antioch, Jerusalem, and Constantinople. More importantly, they defined the doctrines of the Trinity and the Incarnation. The bishops did not presume to say the last word about these mysteries. They merely sought to exclude certain false ways of speaking about the Father, Son, and Holy Spirit.

The councils must be studied in the wider context of the Church Fathers, those highly regarded bishops and writers, the earliest of whom personally knew the Apostles. Tradition includes the decrees of the councils and the writings of the Fathers. It likewise includes the oral formulas of the early Christian preaching (such as the question-and-answer summaries of faith used in the rite of Baptism), apostolic decisions (as at the Council of Jerusalem discussed in Acts 15), interpretations, and customs traceable to apostolic times (such as infant Baptism and prayers for the dead).

Tradition is closely connected to the Sacred Liturgy, the Church's life of worship. Before the New Testament was complete, the apostolic preaching went on, often within the celebration of the Eucharist. In the liturgy, Christ comes in word and sacrament to feed and transform His people. The Fathers of the Second Vatican Council described the Eucharistic Liturgy as the "summit toward which the activity of the Church is directed; it is also the fount from which all her power flows." [166] There is more to the Christian life than the liturgy, of course, but the liturgy

---

[166] Second Vatican Council, Constitution on the Sacred Liturgy, *Sacrosanctum Concilium*, no. 10; cf. Dogmatic Constitution on the Church *Lumen Gentium*, no. 11.

should permeate the life of the Christian. Immersion in the waters of Baptism, anointings with oil, the words of Scripture and creed, the sign of the cross, Christ's self-giving in the Sacrament of the Altar—we might say, with Dom Prosper Guéranger, that the liturgy is "Tradition itself at its highest degree of power and solemnity."[167]

Disputes inevitably arise over conflicting interpretations of God's Word. The Church, as "the pillar and bulwark of the truth,"[168] must be capable of discerning true doctrine and setting it forth clearly. Catholics believe that the Church's teaching authority is invested in the pope, who is the successor of Saint Peter, and the bishops in union with the pope. To the Apostles under Peter and to their successors under the pope, Christ promised the gift of infallibility,[169] which ensures that the Church will never invoke her full teaching authority to require the faithful to believe anything in faith and morals that is false. Aided by the Holy Spirit,[170] the Magisterium authoritatively guides the developed and living Tradition.

From here, we shall focus on the first four ecumenical councils. These dealt with controversies resulting in the earliest, and in some cases enduring, schisms from the Catholic Church.

Nestorianism and the "Church of the East"

The first ecumenical council was held at Nicaea in present-day Turkey in the year A.D. 325. Its main work was the condemnation of Arianism, a heresy named after the priest of Alexandria in Egypt who denied the divinity of the Son. To protect the unity of the divine nature, Arius placed the Son among created beings: a superior creature, a demigod even, but nevertheless most definitely a member of the creaturely realm. The First Council of Nicaea rejected this position, declaring in the creed it drew up that the Son is "begotten, not made, consubstantial with the Father." That is to say, the Son of God is Himself God and there-

---

[167] Prosper Guéranger, *Institutions Liturgiques*, 2 vols (Paris: Débécourt, and Le Mans: Fleuriot, 1840), 1:3.

[168] 1 Timothy 3:15.

[169] Matthew 16:15–19.

[170] See John 16:13.

fore uncreated; for only if Christ be fully God, the Council answered, can He atone for sins and redeem the human race.

The work of Nicaea was taken up by the second ecumenical council in A.D. 381 at Constantinople, the capital of the Eastern Roman, or Byzantine, Empire. This Council expanded the Nicene Creed, developing in particular the teaching on the Holy Spirit, whose divinity it affirmed. By this time, Arianism posed no major threat except in parts of Western Europe, where it met strong opposition—chiefly from Saints Hilary of Poitiers, Martin of Tours, and Ambrose of Milan—and was ultimately eradicated.

The next major theological controversy, this time centering on the Incarnate Lord, was addressed at the Council of Ephesus in A.D. 431. Saint Cyril, Patriarch of Alexandria, and John Nestorius, Patriarch of Constantinople, were key figures at this, the third ecumenical council. Both bishops embraced the Nicene faith, but they diverged in their method of explaining the union of divinity and humanity in Jesus Christ. Nestorius distinguished so emphatically between the two that he seemed to be saying that Christ is two persons, the divine Son and the man Jesus, coexisting in the same body. Cyril, conversely, stressed the fusion of Christ's divinity and humanity. Either approach could lead to heresy if pressed too far. The lack of a shared technical vocabulary made things all the more precarious, as Greek philosophical terms such as "essence," "hypostasis," and "person" were hurled about by people who assigned them different meanings.

Nestorius precipitated the debate by refusing to call the Virgin Mary *Theotokos*, meaning "God-bearer" or "Mother of God." Although this title was already accepted in popular devotion, Nestorius thought it confused Christ's humanity and divinity, thus opening the door to seemingly absurd claims such as that God was born, suffered, and died.[171] Consequently, Nestorius was willing to attribute to Mary the title *Christotokos*, Christ-bearer, but not Theotokos. Cyril countered that Mary is truly God's mother because she bore one of the Trinity: the Word be-

---

[171] "Seemingly" is the operative word because, through what is technically known as the *communicatio idiomatum,* what is said of one Person of the Trinity can be attributed to the Triune God as a whole. Hence, it is correct to say: "God, in Christ, suffered and died."

came flesh for our salvation. Jesus is not a man conjoined to God but a single and undivided Person, God the Son, who assumed our human nature. Cyril won the day at Ephesus; Nestorius was condemned and deposed.

Because Church and State were closely linked at that time, especially in the Byzantine world, theological issues were highly politicized. The Christians of the Persian Empire, Byzantium's enemy to the east, decreed that Nestorius' Christology was in accord with the view always held by their ancient community. Thus it was that the Church of the East, as this community was commonly known, parted with the rest of the Christian fellowship.

Cut off from Catholic unity and wholly wed to Nestorianism, the Church of the East flourished nonetheless. Its theological school in Nisibis, famous for such luminaries as Saint Ephrem the Syrian (*ca.* 306–373), continued to nurture scholars and monks, poets and hermits. After the Arab conquest of Persia in A.D. 637, Nestorian scholars introduced their inquisitive rulers to Greek astronomy, mathematics, and philosophy. Over the next few centuries, Nestorian missionaries traveled far and wide across Asia, penetrating into China and Mongolia. At its zenith in the thirteenth century, the Church of the East claimed more than thirty metropolitan sees and 200 suffragan dioceses. Prior to the Portuguese arrival in India in 1498, Nestorians bolstered the isolated Christian community founded there (according to legend) by the Apostle Thomas, providing bishops for the "Saint Thomas Christians." Dynastic troubles and the upheavals of civil war ultimately wiped out the Church of the East in China, but the Italian Jesuit priest Matteo Ricci, while traveling through China in 1608, encountered a faithful remnant of Nestorians.

Mongol invasions in the fourteenth century and later persecutions have reduced this once mighty Church, which today styles itself the "Holy Apostolic Catholic Assyrian Church of the East," to small communities primarily in Iraq, Iran, Syria, Lebanon, and southern India. In the sixteenth century a portion of the Church of the East reestablished communion with the Bishop of Rome while retaining its ancient East Syrian liturgy and customs, forming the Chaldean Catholic Church, now centered in Baghdad.

An historic meeting of the head of the Assyrian Church, Mar Dinkha IV, and Pope John Paul II took place at Rome in November 1994 and a joint Christological Declaration was signed. Both Churches recognized the other's Christology as not only orthodox but actually the same, albeit expressed in different terms. As to the abovementioned Marian titles, the Declaration states: "We both recognize the legitimacy and rightness of these expressions of the same faith, and we both respect the preference of each Church in her liturgical life and piety." The Assyrian Church and its Chaldean Catholic counterpart have since pledged pastoral cooperation, including the drafting of a common catechism and the establishment of a joint seminary. With the full reintegration of the two communions in God's good time, Christianity's oldest extant schism will at last have ended.

Monophysitism and the "Oriental Orthodox" Churches

The Council of Ephesus (431) endorsed Saint Cyril's affirmation of Mary as *Theotokos*, "Mother of God," thereby safeguarding the unity of Christ's Person. Pressing Cyril's teaching to extremes, the Byzantine monk Eutyches, who had distinguished himself at Ephesus on the Catholic side, maintained that in Christ there not only is a single personality but also a single nature, a divine nature. That is to say, Christ has no human nature: He is "consubstantial" with the Father (and the Holy Spirit) but not with us. This idea, the polar opposite of Nestorianism, is called Monophysitism, from the Greek *mono*, "single," and *physis*, "nature."

Monophysitism was condemned at the Church's fourth ecumenical council, held in 451 at Chalcedon (a suburb of Constantinople, across the Bosphorus) and attended by about six hundred thirty bishops. Taking up the work begun at Ephesus, the Council of Chalcedon taught that Jesus Christ is a single Divine Person, namely, God the Son, possessing both a divine and human nature. The Chalcedonian formula ("two natures, one person"), forged under the influence of Pope Saint Leo the Great (reigned 440–461), affirms the full divinity and full humanity of the Savior.

As so often, cultural and national tensions made theological disputes more bitter. The Christians in Persia, we noted, adopted the Nestorian heresy partially because of Persian opposition to the Byzantine Empire. Similarly, the Monophysite heresy became the national religion of Egypt and Syria, and later Ethiopia and Armenia, because these nations resented the religious and political power of Greek Constantinople. Had it not been for these non-theological factors, the two sides might perhaps have reached a theological agreement after Chalcedon.

In any event, entire communities broke communion with the Catholic Church as a result of their rejection of the doctrine of Chalcedon. These bodies, known collectively as the "Oriental Orthodox" Churches, number approximately 30 million faithful. We should not confuse them with the "Eastern Orthodox" (or simply "Orthodox") Churches, which accept the Council of Chalcedon. The Oriental Orthodox Churches are these: the *Armenian Apostolic Church*; the *Coptic Orthodox Church* in Egypt, the largest Christian community in the Middle East; the *Ethiopian Orthodox Tewahedo Church* (*Tewahedo* is Ge'ez for "unified," a reference to the union of divinity and humanity in one nature); the *Eritrean Orthodox Tewahedo Church*, established following Eritrea's independence from Ethiopia in 1993; the *Syrian Orthodox Church* of Antioch; and the *Malankara Orthodox Syrian Church* in India (also called the *Orthodox Syrian Church of the East*.) [172]

A detailed treatment of these communities is beyond our scope.[173] For our purpose, it is enough to highlight a few facts.

First, the Monophysites, like the Catholics and Eastern Orthodox, have a developed sacramental system, a sacrificial understanding of the Eucharist, bishops in apostolic succession, elaborate rites and ceremonies, monasticism, veneration of the Blessed Virgin Mary and the saints—in short, what we may call a "high" view of the Church.

Second, the Monophysites were great missionaries, like the Nestorians.

Third, as with the Nestorian Church, so also portions of each of the historic Monophysite communities reunited with the

---

[172] Nearly half of India's Monophysite Christians belong to the Malankara Orthodox Syrian Church, while the other half makes up (note the word order) the Malankara Syrian Orthodox Church, which is under the jurisdiction of the Syrian Orthodox Patriarch of Antioch.

[173] Much information about their histories, traditions, liturgical rites, and demographics is available on the website of the Catholic Near East Welfare Association, *www.cnewa.org*, which also provides links to these Churches' official websites.

Catholic Church at various times while retaining their own customs and rites. Thus we have the Armenian, Coptic, Ethiopian, Syrian, and Syro-Malankara Catholic Churches—all espousing the teachings of Chalcedon, and all in union with the Bishop of Rome.

Finally, scholars now generally agree that the difference between Monophysites and "Chalcedonians" was basically one of terminology, not of theology. Recall that in the fourth and fifth centuries, the bishops and theologians assembled in general council lacked a standard philosophical vocabulary for resolving the controversies of the day. The Monophysite schism, like the Nestorian, has now been resolved in principle, and full reunion between these separated Eastern Churches and their smaller Catholic counterparts is within reach.

To sum up, neither Nestorianism nor Monophysitism, in their conventional meanings, expresses the full truth about the Incarnation. Nestorianism, in dividing Christ into two persons, would have us believe, for instance, that the "I" speaking when Jesus said, "I thirst" was different from the "I" who said, "Before Abraham was, I am." Conversely, in confusing Christ into one nature, Monophysitism unwittingly loses His Sacred Humanity in His Divinity, as a drop of wine is swallowed up in the ocean. Each of these theories finds its counterweight in Catholicism, which integrates the faith of Nicaea and Constantinople, of Ephesus and Chalcedon, thus upholding the fullness of the truth about Him who is at once fully God and fully human.

The Orthodox Church

The divisions that have resulted in the present fragmentation of Christianity occurred in three main stages, at intervals of roughly five hundred years. We have already studied the first stage, when in the fifth and sixth centuries the Church in Persia adopted the Nestorian heresy and the majority of Christians in Egypt, Ethiopia, Syria, and Armenia embraced Monophysitism.

Then came the second separation, the so-called Great Schism, conventionally dated to the year 1054. Political, social, cultural, and religious forces had long been pulling Eastern and Western Christianity apart. From the time of the Council of Chalcedon

(451) when Pope Saint Leo the Great rejected its Canon 28, which granted great jurisdictional powers to Constantinople, relations between Rome and Constantinople were marked by occasional episodes of high tension. The Great Schism was primarily a sundering of the Western or "Latin" Church, centered on Rome, from the Eastern or "Greek" Church, centered on Constantinople; the other three Eastern patriarchates had by this time been greatly diminished and isolated under Muslim domination. Christendom now became divided into two communions: in the West, the "Catholic Church" under the pope in Rome; and in the Byzantine Empire, the "Orthodox Church" of the East. Both claim to be the true Catholic Church.

The third separation, which came with the Protestant Reformation in the sixteenth century, will be addressed later.

Our concern now is the Great Schism and the communion of 200 million Christians that calls itself the Orthodox Church. This body is in fact not a unitary Church but a federation of independent local Churches, joined by sharing the same faith, the same sacraments, and, one is tempted to say, an historic antipathy toward Rome. There is within Orthodoxy no one bishop with an equivalent position to the pope in Catholicism. The Patriarch of Constantinople (since 1991, Bartholomew I), also known as the Ecumenical Patriarch, enjoys a position of special honor as "the first among equals" (a position once accorded to the pope), but he has no right to interfere in the affairs of the Churches outside his patriarchate. Today the Patriarchate of Constantinople includes the few thousand Greeks living in Turkey as well as some parts of Greece.

Since Orthodoxy has no permanent center of authority and unity, we cannot define the Orthodox Church as all those in communion with the Church of Constantinople, in the way that we may legitimately define the Catholic Church as all those in communion with the Church of Rome. As far as the Orthodox are concerned, the Church of Constantinople could lapse from Orthodox unity tomorrow, just as (in their view) the Church of Rome did a millennium ago.

Orthodoxy's primary area of distribution lies in Eastern Europe, in Russia, and along the coasts of the eastern Mediterranean. There are presently fourteen Orthodox Churches that are generally recognized as "autocephalous" (from Greek, "self-headed"). Highest in honor among these are the four ancient patriarchates of Constantinople, Alexandria, Antioch, and Jerusalem (Rome having "lapsed" in 1054). All of these, together with Rome, claim apostolic foundation and, with the exception of Jerusalem, were the most important cities in the Roman Empire. The other ten autocephalous Churches have emerged over the centuries in Cyprus (established in 434), Georgia (466), Bulgaria (927), Serbia (1219), Russia (1589), Greece (1850), Poland (1924), Romania (1925), Albania (1937), and the former Czechoslovakia (1951).[174] In 1970 the Patriarchate of Moscow, on its own initiative, granted autocephalous status to most of its parishes in North America under the name of the Orthodox Church in America (OCA); but because the Ecumenical Patriarchate of Constantinople claims the exclusive right to grant independence, it and most other Orthodox Churches do not recognize the autocephaly of the OCA. The heads of the Russian, Romanian, Serbian, Bulgarian, and Georgian Churches are known by the title Patriarch; the heads of the other Churches are called Archbishop or Metropolitan.

Several Churches, while self-governing in most respects, are not fully independent and are therefore termed "autonomous" but not "autocephalous." The Orthodox Church of Sinai (effectively, the monastery of Saint Catherine there) is dependent on the Jerusalem Patriarchate; the Orthodox Church of Finland and the Estonian Apostolic Orthodox Church are under the jurisdiction of the Ecumenical Patriarchate; and the Estonian Orthodox Church is under the Patriarchate of Moscow. The Moscow Patriarchate has granted independent status to its daughter Churches in China and Japan, but these actions have not been recognized by Constantinople.

Additionally, there are Churches deemed "un-canonical" or illegitimate by Orthodoxy as a whole, such as the Belorussian and Macedonian Churches, and the two entities vying with each other and with the canonical Ukrainian Orthodox Church (which is loyal to the Moscow Patriarchate) for the allegiance of Orthodox Christians in Ukraine, namely, the Ukrainian Autocephalous

---

[174] In 1993 Czechoslovakia peacefully split into two independent nations: the Czech Republic (consisting of Bohemia and Moravia) and Slovakia.

Orthodox Church and the Ukrainian Orthodox Church–Kiev Patriarchate. Most Ukrainian Orthodox living outside Ukraine are under the spiritual care of Constantinople, which has never accepted the unilateral forced subordination of the Ukrainian Orthodox Church to Moscow in 1686.[175]

The relationship between Western and Eastern Christians since the Great Schism reads like a tragic romance story: attraction and hunger for unity, urges and rivalry, misunderstanding and confusion. Let us now examine Orthodox Christian belief and practice, attending especially to the theological and historical issues that contributed to this millennium-old breach.

A Gradual Estrangement

The faith of Orthodox Christians agrees in the vast majority of points with that of Catholics. In fact, Orthodox and Catholics have so much in common that it can be tempting to think of Orthodoxy as a kind of Catholicism without the pope. Orthodox Christians accept all the books of the Bible that Catholics accept. Their worship is centered on the same seven sacraments. They use the Nicene-Constantinopolitan Creed and understand every word of it, but for one clause, just as Catholics do. They believe, as Catholics believe, in a visible Church with authority to teach and to make laws. With Catholics, they venerate and pray to the Mother of God and the saints. And Orthodox bishops, like Catholic bishops, are ordained in apostolic succession to be the ongoing presence and voice of the Apostles.

"Between the Catholic Church and the Orthodox Church," observes Father Neuhaus, "there are powerful continuities of apostolic ministry, doctrine, and devotion that bind us together in our division."[176] Because of these "powerful continuities," Catholic catechesis has traditionally distinguished between Orthodox and Protestant Christianity by declaring the former to be only in schism from Rome while describing the latter as heretically separated.

[175] A great deal of information about the various Orthodox Churches is available at the website of the Catholic Near East Welfare Association, *www.cnewa.org*, which also provides links to these Churches' official websites.

[176] Richard John Neuhaus, "Reconciling East and West," *First Things* 188 (December 2008): 23–28, at p. 23.

What, then, divides Catholicism and Orthodoxy? There are two chief controversies, which are more closely related than would seem. One is the primacy of the pope, that is to say his authority, as successor of Saint Peter, over all the Churches. The other is the relation of the Holy Spirit to the Father and Son. Before taking up these questions, it will help to consider the gradual estrangement of the Christian East and Christian West, which culminated in open and formal schism in 1054. This background can point the way through the differences that divide us.

Although the fundamental cause of the schism was theological, it was conditioned by cultural and political influences that had distanced East and West long before the dawn of the second millennium. From the end of the third century, the Roman Empire was divided into an eastern and western part, each under its own emperor. As was noted, the Eastern Roman Empire is what historians call the Byzantine Empire, or Byzantium. It extended as far north as the Slavic lands and created its own Greco-Roman world that distinguished itself from the Latin Europe of the West.

Alongside "Old Rome" on the Tiber was the new imperial capital in the East, Constantinople, the "New Rome" on the Bosphorus. Constantinople, with its patriarch and imperial court, was, in the view of many, the center of Christendom. The Byzantine emperors were regarded as temporal representatives of the eternal rule of Christ the heavenly King, and they sometimes did more for the Church than bishops to mediate religious conflicts and provide for the flourishing of the Christian community. The bishops, for their part, had the responsibility and power of judging the theological orthodoxy of the emperor.

Barbarian invasions in the fifth century destroyed what little remained of the political unity of Greek East and Latin West. The rise of Islam a few centuries later furthered the severance: the Mediterranean now passed largely into Arab control, and contacts between the Latins and Byzantines became far more difficult. Cut off from Byzantium, the West proceeded to set up its own empire. On Christmas Day in the year 800, Pope Leo III crowned Charlemagne, the Frankish king, as Emperor of the Holy Roman Empire. The East regarded the papal coronation as an act of schism within the Empire.

Problems of language made matters worse. In the first few centuries of the Christian era, educated people throughout the Empire could speak and write both Latin and Greek. By the sixth century, however, few Western Europeans knew Greek and few Byzantines spoke Latin. East and West no longer drew upon the same sources nor read the same literature. Each side remained enclosed in its own world of ideas and did little to meet each other half way. Consequently, theology as a discipline developed along different paths in East and West. Examples abound. Latin thought was influenced by the concepts of Roman law, while the Greeks understood theology primarily in the light of the Sacred Liturgy. When thinking about the Trinity, Latins started with God's unity, Greeks with God's tri-personality. Latins spoke more of redemption, Greeks of deification. Latin piety focused on Christ the Victim, Greek piety on Christ the Victor. Both approaches are complementary and have their place in the fullness of Tradition, but now there was a danger that each side would follow its own approach in isolation, forgetting the value in the other's perspective.

Papal primacy and the "procession" of the Holy Spirit are two points where the two sides no longer complemented each other but entered into conflict. Despite the various factors that increasingly divided East and West, visible unity in the one Catholic Church might still have been preserved, had there not been these two further points of contention.

From Estrangement to Schism

Differences in language and culture aggravated by a lack of communications led to continuing estrangement between the patriarchates of the East, what is today known as the Orthodox Church, and the Catholic Church of the West. Historians typically identify two flashpoints in this gradual parting of ways. First came the conflict, in 863, between Pope Saint Nicholas I and Patriarch Photius of Constantinople (known in Orthodoxy as Saint Photius the Great) over whether Photius legitimately occupied the patriarchal throne. Communion between the Churches of Rome and Constantinople was temporarily broken, and although Photius in his second period of office (877–886) remained in communion with Rome, no solution was found to the underlying causes of the conflict. Then came a further clash in 1054, when Cardinal Humbert and two other papal legates traveled to Constantinople on what was meant to be a mission of reconciliation. Things went so badly that sentences of excommunication were leveled against the patriarch Michael Cerularius and two other persons by the papal legates, who in turn were declared excommunicate by Michael. In 1965, Pope Paul VI and Ecumenical Patriarch Athenagoras revoked these mutual excommunications.

As significant as these events are, they are parts of a much more complex story that begins well before the ninth century and continues long after 1054. More divisive than anything previous was the sacking of Constantinople by the Fourth Crusaders in 1204, which introduced a new spirit of hatred. Orthodox bishop Timothy (Kallistos) Ware remarks, with stunning understatement: "As the Byzantines watched the Crusaders tear to pieces the altar and icon screen in the Church of the Holy Wisdom, and set prostitutes on the Patriarch's throne, they must have felt that those who did such things were not Christians in the same sense as themselves." [177]

Although reunion was proclaimed at two councils attended by the Orthodox, Lyons (1274) and Florence (1438–39), in each case this remained no more than an agreement on paper, for the decisions were rejected by the vast majority of Orthodox clergy and laity. Nevertheless, friendly relations between Orthodox and Catholics continued in some areas as late as the eighteenth century. For example, Orthodox bishops frequently invited the Jesuits to preach, hear confessions, and open schools. Were we to assign a specific date to the "final" breach, then probably the year should be 1724, when a schism occurred in the Church of Antioch between pro-papal and anti-papal groups, and rival patriarchs were elected. Whatever doors had remained open were now slammed shut.

We come now to the two fundamental issues in the schism between Rome and the Eastern Churches. The first has to do with the "procession," or "going forth from," of the Holy Spirit. When

[177] Timothy Ware, *The Orthodox Church* (New York: Viking Penguin, 1963; rev. ed. 1983), p. 69.

both sides speak of the Spirit's procession, they refer not to God's outward action toward creation (the sending of the Spirit to the world) but to the relations existing *within* the Trinity before creation existed. God is triune from all eternity. No work of creation or redemption was needed for the Father to beget a Son who is His perfect Image and Word; no prophecy or sanctification of souls was required for the mutual love of Father and Son to breathe forth the Holy Spirit.

Yet the mystery of God's inner life is so impenetrable that human words can never be adequate to the task. Accordingly, two ways of speaking of the Spirit's procession came about. The Latin tradition holds that the Spirit proceeds from the Father *and* the Son as from a single "principle" or origin, whereas the Greek tradition holds that the Spirit proceeds from the Father *through* the Son. For centuries this difference was not controversial, much less a cause for schism. It first became a problem when, in the West, the word *filioque* ("and from the Son") was added to the Nicene-Constantinopolitan Creed. The change originated in Spain in the fifth to seventh centuries, probably as a safeguard against Arianism (which, to recall, denied the Son's divinity), but was not adopted at Rome until 1014. The Orthodox use the creed in its original form, professing that the Spirit "proceeds from the Father."

It was writers at Charlemagne's court who first made the *filioque* a matter of controversy, accusing the Greeks of heresy because they used the unaltered creed. In turn, the Greeks denounced the *filioque* as theologically unsound, even heretical, for it seems to compromise the Father's role as sole fountainhead of the Trinity. They further protested the unilateral alteration of the creed. In place of the *filioque*, Patriarch Photius set the formula "from the Father alone," brushing aside the favored phrase of the Greek Fathers and rendering impossible any agreement with the Latins.

The second main point of conflict concerns papal authority. Barbarian invasions and the collapse of the Roman Empire in the West greatly contributed to the centralization of the Latin Church. By force of circumstances, the popes assumed a part which the Eastern bishops never played: they became monarchs set up over Christendom, commanding both ecclesiastical subordinates and secular rulers. Moreover, they claimed jurisdiction over all the Churches, not only in the West but also in the East. The Greeks accorded the Bishop of Rome a primacy of honor, together with the right to hear appeals from all parts of the Church, but they would not acknowledge him as "universal pontiff." Accordingly, Catholicism teaches that the pope enjoys pastoral jurisdiction over the whole Church, while Orthodoxy does not believe any bishop to be endowed with universal jurisdiction.

We will continue to look at these and lesser points of difference between the Catholic and Orthodox Churches, considering also some possibilities for deepening their existing unity in the truth revealed by Christ.

Orthodox Belief and Worship

Besides the *"Filioque"* controversy and the papal claims, lesser matters of worship and discipline caused trouble between the Western and Eastern Churches, once two parts of a single communion. The Greeks allowed married priests (but not married bishops), the Latins required clerical celibacy; the Greeks used leavened bread for the Eucharist, the Latins used unleavened bread ("azymes"); the Greeks and Latins had different laws of fasting; and so forth. Still, there is much more that unites than divides the two great communions.

We focus now on the worship of the Orthodox Church. "Orthodoxy" literally means both "right belief" and "right worship," being derived from two Greek words: *orthos* (correct) and *doxa* (glory, worship, doctrine). Because of their common apostolic heritage, Orthodox and Catholics agree that the chief place in Christian worship belongs to the sacraments—or, as Eastern Christians call them, the "mysteries." The Orthodox Church speaks customarily of seven sacraments, the same seven as in Catholic theology: Baptism, Chrismation (equivalent to Confirmation in the West), the Holy Eucharist, Repentance or Confession, Holy Orders, Matrimony, and the Anointing of the Sick.

In Orthodoxy, as in the early Church, the three sacraments of Christian initiation—Baptism, Chrismation, and the Eucharist—

are closely linked together. Orthodox children are not only baptized in infancy but also confirmed and given Communion in infancy—a strong testimony to the fact that *all* the sacraments are divine gifts, not merited by age or training.

Except in emergencies, Orthodoxy regards Baptism by immersion as essential, because Baptism signifies a burial and resurrection with Christ,[178] and the outward sign of this is the plunging of the candidate into the font, followed by his emergence from the water. Hence, Orthodox are troubled by the fact that Western Christianity is, in most instances, content to pour a little water over the candidate's forehead. As they see it, pouring—or worse, sprinkling—undercuts, certainly not the validity of the sacrament, but the sacramental symbolism. After all, does not Roman Catholic theology itself teach that sacramental rites should accurately symbolize the spiritual realities they convey?

Whereas in the West it is the bishop who normally confirms, in the East Chrismation is administered by a priest, who takes a special ointment, the sacred chrism (in Greek, *myron*), which has been blessed by a bishop, and with this he anoints various parts of the child's body, marking them with the sign of the cross. Like Catholics, Orthodox believe that Confirmation is an extension of Pentecost: the same Holy Spirit who descended visibly on the Apostles in tongues of fire now descends invisibly on the baptized.

As regards the Eucharist, the laity as well as the clergy always receive Holy Communion under both species. Communion is given to the laity in a spoon, containing a small piece of the consecrated bread together with a portion of the consecrated wine; it is always received standing. Both Catholics and Orthodox believe that the Eucharist is truly the Body and Blood of Christ, although they understand the "moment of consecration" somewhat differently. According to Latin theology, dating to about the twelfth century, the consecration is brought about solely by the words of institution: "This is my Body," "This is . . . my Blood."[179] While not denying the efficacy of those words, Orthodox theology follows the earlier common tradition of East

[178] See Romans 6:4–5; Colossians 2:12.
[179] Cf. Matthew 26:26–29; Mark 14:22–25; Luke 22:19–21; 1 Corinthians 11:24–25.

and West in regarding the entire *anaphora*, or Eucharistic Prayer, and not just one part of it, as consecratory.

The Orthodox Church, like the Catholic Church, teaches that the Eucharist is not only a sacrament but also a sacrifice—indeed none other than Christ's sacrifice—offered to God for the world's salvation. Bishop Ware explains the Orthodox position in terms that fully accord with Catholic doctrine:

> The Eucharist is not a bare commemoration nor an imaginary representation of Christ's sacrifice, but the true sacrifice itself; yet on the other hand it is not a new sacrifice, nor a repetition of the sacrifice on Calvary, since the Lamb was sacrificed "once only, for all time." The events of Christ's sacrifice—the Incarnation, the Last Supper, the Crucifixion, the Resurrection, the Ascension—are not repeated in the Eucharist, but they are *made present*.[180]

Although the Latin and Eastern Churches have differed for many centuries and in many respects regarding the sacraments of initiation, both sides teach that Christian initiation is a unity in which Confirmation is the perfection of Baptism and the Eucharist is the completion of both. Therefore, the fact that in the West a baptized child will normally receive the Eucharist years before being confirmed is, to put it mildly, an anomaly.

Of great importance to Orthodox piety are icons—images of Christ, the Virgin Mary, the saints, and biblical events, often painted on wood with a gold leaf background, and kept and venerated both in churches and in private homes. These holy images, together with frescoes and mosaics—Orthodox churches generally do not have statues—are not mere ornaments designed to add warmth and color to the church, but have a theological and liturgical function. What the Gospel is to the ears, icons are to the eyes. What is more, icons remind the Orthodox faithful of

---

[180] Ware, *The Orthodox Church*, pp. 293–94, emphasis in original. In 1562, the Catholic Church at the Council of Trent taught that the Mass is a representation (literally, a making present), a memorial, and an application of Jesus Christ's unique (and so unrepeatable) sacrifice of the Cross (Session 22, *Doctrine on the Most Holy Sacrifice of the Mass*). Toward the middle of the twentieth century, theologians began to speak of Christ's whole life-process, not only His Passion, as a sacrifice, inasmuch as His death was the last and dramatic expression of what had been a life of continual self-offering in love to the Father.

another truth that they profess with Catholics, namely, that the liturgy on earth is one with the heavenly liturgy.

The basic pattern of the liturgy—the official public worship of the Church as distinguished from private prayers and devotions—is the same in Orthodoxy as in Catholicism. There is, above all, the Eucharistic Sacrifice or Mass, which Eastern Christians call the "Divine Liturgy," together with the other sacraments; second, the Divine Office, a collection of psalms, prayers and hymns recited at certain times of the day; and third, services intended for special occasions such as monastic profession, the consecration of a church, and burial of the dead.

Beginning in the thirteenth century, the patriarchs of Constantinople pressured all Orthodox churches to adopt the Byzantine Rite, which had originated as the rite of the cathedral of Constantinople, Hagia Sophia (Holy Wisdom). As this rite spread throughout the East, it displaced the older rites previously celebrated by the local churches. (Similarly, in the Latin Church from about the eighth century, the Roman Rite became gradually more widespread, replacing or assimilating local rites wherever it was introduced.) Only those Eastern Churches that were not in communion with Constantinople—the Nestorians and Monophysites—were able to maintain their ancient rites. In theory, however, Orthodoxy does not require exclusive adherence to the Byzantine Rite, any more than Catholicism requires exclusive use of the Roman Rite.

In most Orthodox churches, the sanctuary is separated from the main body of the church, or nave, by a solid screen called an *iconostasis*, having three openings: the "Royal Doors" in the center and two smaller side doors called "Deacons' Doors." The Royal Doors bear the image of the Annunciation, for it was by passing through the Virgin Mary's womb that God the Word took flesh, passing from Heaven to earth that He might lead us from earth to Heaven. The four Evangelists are often depicted on the doors as heralds of the Gospel.

Flanking the Royal Doors are icons of Christ and His Mother on the viewer's right and left respectively. Next to Christ is an icon of Saint John the Baptist, "the greatest of all born of woman," [181] who

---

[181] Lauded as such by Jesus (Matthew 11:11).

heralded the Lord's coming. Adjacent to the icon of the Virgin is an icon of the church's patron saint.

On the Deacons' Doors appear either the holy angels or deacon-saints. If the sanctuary represents Heaven and the nave earth, the role of the angels and deacons are parallel. The angels go back and forth between Heaven and earth as the deacons go back and forth between the altar and the nave. As the angels are God's messengers and our heavenly intercessors, the deacons who stand before the doors leading the people in prayer are like angels knocking on the gates of Paradise.

Over the Royal Doors is located an image of the "Mystical Supper," or Last Supper. A crucifixion icon marks the pinnacle of the iconostasis. In Slavic countries, the iconostasis becomes even more elaborate, with prophets and ancestors of Christ and rows of interceding saints. Thus, the iconostasis displays the entire preparation and accomplishment of our salvation. Although it separates the nave from the altar, it is considered a barrier only by those who are ignorant of its true function as a visible sign of the union of Heaven and earth. The vines, medallions, and peacocks found on some iconostases symbolize the redeemed Garden of Paradise, the destiny of all the faithful.

The Divine Liturgy is structured around a series of appearances of the sacred ministers from behind the iconostasis. The most important of these appearances are the two solemn entrances. The "Little Entrance," after the opening rite, is a procession with the Gospel Book, symbolizing Christ's coming to us in the Word; the other, "Great Entrance" at the beginning of the Eucharistic part of the service, is a procession bearing to the altar the gifts of bread and wine prepared before the beginning of the Liturgy; this is said to prefigure Christ's coming to us in the Eucharist. Both these anticipations are fulfilled in two later appearances: the procession of the deacon with the Gospel to the ambo for the reading, and the procession of the celebrant to distribute Communion.

The Byzantine Rite features three forms of the Divine Liturgy throughout the year: the Liturgy of Saint John Chrysostom (used most Sundays), the Liturgy of Saint Basil the Great (used ten times a year), and, rarest, the Liturgy of Saint James, celebrated in certain places only on Saint James' Day, October 23. There is also the Liturgy of the Presanctified, used on Wednesdays and Fridays in Lent, and on the first three days of Holy Week. This liturgy contains no Eucharistic consecration and sacrifice; instead, Communion is given from elements consecrated at the previous Sunday's Divine Liturgy.

While in most Catholic parishes and chapels the Eucharist is celebrated daily, in the Orthodox Church a daily Divine Liturgy is unusual except in cathedrals and large monasteries. In a normal parish church it is celebrated only on Sundays and feasts. In contrast to the sobriety and comparative brevity of Roman Catholic liturgy, the Byzantine liturgy is florid, opulent, and lengthy. There is no Byzantine equivalent to the "Low Mass." At every Divine Liturgy, incense is used and the service is sung, even if there be no choir or congregation, but only the priest and a single server or reader. Instrumental music is prohibited except in some Greek Orthodox churches in America.

Having treated thus far the sacraments of Christian initiation and the Divine Liturgy, we will now touch briefly on other aspects of Orthodox sacramental life.

Almost Full Communion

If the prevailing practice in Latin-rite Catholicism of administering the Eucharist to unconfirmed children departs from the older, common tradition of East and West, so, from the Catholic viewpoint, Orthodox sacramental life has its irregularities, too. For instance, under some circumstances the Orthodox Church permits divorce and remarriage even in the case of a consummated sacramental marriage, citing as its authority Matthew 19:9, which it takes as an exception to Christ's general ruling about the indissolubility of marriage.[182] The Catholic Church recognizes that unconsummated sacramental marriages can be dissolved for weighty reasons, but does not recognize the possibility of remarriage in the case of consummated sacramental marriages as long as both spouses are living. Despite the

---

[182] Matthew 19:9: "And I say to you: whoever divorces his wife, except for unchastity, and marries another, commits adultery; and he who marries a divorced woman, commits adultery."

conflicting approaches, neither side has ever officially accused the other of erring in its teaching on this matter. Parenthetically, both Churches agree that a Christian marriage must be sealed in the Church and not before a civil magistrate; but whereas the Orthodox Church holds that the priest is minister of the sacrament, the Catholic Church regards the partners as ministers of the sacrament, the priest (or deacon) being the Church's official witness.

Orthodox theology is intensely conservative and, when confronted with Western theological developments, even reactionary. A particular manifestation of this is the Orthodox attitude toward the Catholic doctrine of the Immaculate Conception, according to which the Virgin Mary, from the moment she was conceived, was by a special grace of God preserved from original sin. While the Orthodox Church invokes Mary as "all-holy," "immaculate" or "spotless," it has never formally pronounced on the doctrine. A few Orthodox accept the Catholic definition or something close to it, but most reject it as an innovation, protesting that it stems from a false understanding of original sin, or that it places Mary outside the rest of humanity, or that the Church may legitimately dogmatize only what the Apostles publicly taught.

To be fair, the Immaculate Conception was the subject of much debate during the Middle Ages in the West. Blessed John Duns Scotus championed it; Saint Thomas Aquinas opposed it. The doctrine was not finally defined until 1854. That is because the development of doctrine had not reached the point of comprehending how Mary's preservation from sin could be the result entirely of a future event, namely, Christ's atoning sacrifice on Calvary. It should be remembered that the feast of Our Lady's conception came to us from the East and is observed in all the Eastern Churches. The theological and liturgical texts of the Greeks and Slavs imply the Immaculate Conception plainly enough. And long after the schism of 1054, Orthodox theologians and spiritual writers were teaching the doctrine more and more plainly until Protestant influence gave impetus to an opposing school. These facts invite the suspicion that Orthodoxy came to deny a belief primarily because the Bishop of Rome had formally defined it. Reactionary motives are suggested also by the fact that both the Catholic and Orthodox Churches affirm Mary's bodily Assumption into Heaven and commemorate it on August 15; yet after Pope Pius XII defined the Assumption as a dogma in 1950, some Orthodox began to express doubts about the doctrine and even explicitly to deny it.

Another difference between East and West is the idea of Purgatory (from the Latin *purgare*, to purify). As a point of dispute between the two Churches, this only came into the open in the thirteenth century. While the doctrine is most fully developed in Catholic theology, many Orthodox theologians also affirm a version of it. The doctrine stems from the belief that the souls of persons who die in a state of grace might still have vestiges of sin, which must be removed before they enter a Heaven of perfect love and communion with God.[183] It is rooted also in the popular conviction that prayers avail to help the dead.[184] Catholics have traditionally viewed Purgatory as a state of temporal punishment and expiation of sins not fully repented of, whereas Orthodox see it as a process of growth and maturation toward full transformation in Christ. Either way, the main idea is sanctification after death, and perhaps the doctrine of Purgatory really asserts nothing more.

Papal primacy and infallibility, the procession of the Holy Spirit, the moment of Eucharistic consecration, the Immaculate Conception, Purgatory: our notice of these and other Orthodox–Catholic points of difference is liable to falsify our proportion. Catholic and Orthodox Christians profess virtually the same faith, celebrate the same sacraments, and claim as their own the undivided Church of the first millennium. Bishop Ware again: "Athanasius and Basil lived in the east, but they belong also to the west; and Orthodox who live in France, Britain, or Ireland can in their turn look upon the national saints of these lands—Alban and Patrick, Cuthbert and Bede, Geneviève of Paris and Augustine of Canterbury—not as strangers but as members of their own Church." [185]

It is gratifying to note that, from the Catholic side at least, most

---

[183] See Revelation 21:27.
[184] See 2 Maccabees 12:46.
[185] Ware, *The Orthodox Church*, p. 10.

of the differences between the two communions need not hinder their reunion. For example, in the Catholic understanding, the *filioque* is not a church-dividing issue,[186] as evidenced by the fact that Eastern-rite Catholic Churches may omit the clause. If, in keeping with the stated purpose of this book, we identify Catholicism rather than Orthodoxy as the fullness of the Christian revelation, it is principally for two reasons to which we now turn.

Catholicity and the Distinctively Catholic

As far as I can tell, there are two—but only two—reasons for identifying Catholicism rather than Orthodoxy as the fullness of the truth that Christ's one Church has been given to guard and teach.

First, the Orthodox Church lacks the divinely willed, visible center of unity that is the papacy. The preeminence of the Church of Rome and her bishop, the pope, is based on a number of historical considerations. In times of persecution, the Roman Church exhibited exceptional fidelity and doctrinal purity. The Apostles Peter and Paul were martyred at Rome. To this must be added the growing persuasion, beginning sporadically in the third century and constantly from the fourth, that in Matthew 16 our Lord gave Saint Peter jurisdiction and teaching authority in the entire Church; Luke 22 and John 21 also clearly accent Peter. Throughout the first millennium, both Latin and Greek theologians acknowledged the transmission of Peter's ministry to the bishops of Rome, whose judgments were held as authoritative. By reducing the pope's primacy to a mere "primacy of honor," which means practically nothing, Orthodoxy has forsaken the Tradition of the undivided Church. A fully adequate understanding of Christ's Church demands also an adequate account of the role of Peter and the Petrine ministry of the Bishop of Rome.

The second reason has to do with Christ's promise, in John 16, to guide the Church into all truth by the help of the Holy Spirit.

---

[186] For the commemoration of the 1500th anniversary of the Council of Constantinople and the 1450th anniversary of the Council of Ephesus, Pope John Paul II and Patriarch Bartholomew I recited the Nicene-Constantinopolitan Creed in Greek at St. Peter's in Rome, omitting the *Filioque* phrase.

Our Lord bequeathed the Gospel to His Apostles, through whom it became the apostolic Tradition of the infant Church. As certain revealed truths impressed themselves more and more deeply on the Church's consciousness, their meaning and implications were fleshed out more fully. Many doctrinal definitions were formulated at the Church's ecumenical councils, as we saw with regard to the divinity of Christ and His two natures. Like any great idea, the truths of revelation live and grow, and because of the guidance of the Holy Spirit, this growth and expression are always in line with the original idea. For centuries, there has been no significant outgrowth of earlier doctrines in Orthodoxy such as Catholicism has known. Rather, Orthodox theology seems stuck in a debilitating reactionary mode. Such bluntness might be taken as condescension but for the fact that many Orthodox acknowledge and even celebrate this lack of continuous development. When they look westward, they see what appears to them a Church distorted by innovation and error.

So, where do we go from here?

Since the Second Vatican Council, the Catholic Church has continued to emphasize the papacy as a visible center of unity while simultaneously ascribing greater importance to the role of bishops than was previously customary. Individual bishops, the council taught, are "the visible principle and foundation of unity in their particular churches."[187] This increased attention to the ministry of bishops, advanced by Popes John Paul II and Benedict XVI, counterbalances the doctrine of the First Vatican Council (1869–1870), which so exalted the papal office that all other bishops were made to seem like branch managers of Rome rather than vicars of Christ in their own right. Whatever else he is, the pope is a bishop among bishops; his universal pastorate need not derogate from the dignity of the other patriarchs and bishops. The Orthodox are understandably gratified to hear Rome describe her primacy as the servant of communion, within a framework of genuine interdependence between the pope and his brother bishops.

Were East and West to reunite, Rome could again serve as the final court of appeal in disputes among bishops and particular

---

[187] Second Vatican Council, Dogmatic Constitution on the Church, *Lumen Gentium*, no. 23.

Churches. Papal leadership might offer the Orthodox world a partial antidote to its fragmentation, which is driven chiefly by extreme nationalism. The Ecumenical Patriarch is powerless to stop this because he lacks any true authority outside his own small community and is seen as the representative of one of the ethnic factions, the Greeks. Papal authority enables the Church to function as an authentically *catholic* (or "universal") body.

Since the nineteenth century, segments of the various Orthodox Churches have come into union with the Church of Rome while maintaining all their traditions, except those that would conflict with Catholic doctrine.[188] These communities retain the name of the Church from which they derive. Those that adhere to the Byzantine liturgical, theological, and spiritual tradition are collectively referred to as "Greek Catholic" because of the Greek origin of the Byzantine Rite; thus we have the Ukrainian Greek-Catholic Church, the Slovak Greek-Catholic Church, the Hungarian Greek-Catholic Church, and so forth—all following the same Byzantine Rite used by the Orthodox Churches. Therefore, we must be careful not to identify Catholicism exclusively with the Catholic Church of the West, the Church of the Latin Rite.

The existence of these Eastern Catholic Churches within traditionally Orthodox lands is an ongoing source of tension between Rome and the Orthodox. In striving to be loyal both to the pope and to their native religious heritage, Eastern Catholics often find themselves between a rock and a hard place, trying to be Catholic in a way most Catholics are not aware of or do not understand, while trying to be Eastern in a way their Orthodox mother Churches deem traitorous. By expanding our vision of Catholicism beyond the limits of our own Western tradition, by discovering and esteeming the spiritual treasures of the East, we can help Eastern-rite Catholics fulfill their difficult vocation; and they, in turn, can show us new ways of living the fullness of Christian faith.

Protestantism

Having now acquainted ourselves with the Eastern Churches—the Assyrian (Nestorian), Oriental Orthodox (Monophysite), and

---

[188] Information about the Catholic Eastern Churches is available at the website of the Catholic Near East Welfare Association, *www.cnewa.org.*

Eastern Orthodox (Chalcedonian)—we turn westward, to the Christian communities born directly or indirectly of the Protestant Reformation of the sixteenth century.

Protestant Christianity is not a single communion but an alphabet soup of denominations, transdenominational fellowships, and independent congregations, most of which today may be categorized as either mainline or evangelical. Mainline Protestantism is historically divided along denominational lines: Lutheran, Episcopalian (Anglican), Methodist, Presbyterian, Congregationalist, Baptist, and others. Many evangelical Protestants belong to independent local churches, while millions of others are affiliated with denominations such as the Assemblies of God, the Southern Baptist Convention (the largest Protestant body in the United States), the Nazarenes, and sundry "Holiness" groups. The term "evangelical" itself covers a vast spectrum of doctrine, discipline, and organization. There are evangelicals who believe in the effective grace of infant Baptism, and others who do not.

With the cultural revolutions of the 1960s, new fault lines emerged in Protestantism. More significant than the old denominational distinctions are the divisions *within* the mainline churches between those who are committed to the historic teachings and practices of their denomination, and those who would accommodate the Gospel to liberal secular culture, especially when it comes to sex and abortion. Serious, believing Lutherans, for example, now typically feel that they have more in common with serious, believing Baptists—with serious, believing Catholics, for that matter—than they do with the progressive members of their own denomination. The mainline church bureaucracies are predominantly liberal in theological commitments and social and political attitudes, whereas evangelical church leadership and laity alike are generally conservative.

Despite their conflicts and contradictions, their organizational divisions and revisions, and—prior to the rise of the ecumenical movement that was launched early in the twentieth century— their history of sermonizing against one another, Protestants have always felt some interdenominational unity because they were all "Protestant," named by their protest against the Church of Rome. To be a Protestant meant chiefly that one was not a

Catholic or Orthodox—although Orthodoxy has never been a significant presence in the minds of most Protestants. For various reasons, many who used to call themselves Protestant now prefer to be known simply as Christian.

The term "Protestant" derives from the protest drawn up by a small group of German princes at the imperial Diet (court) of Speyer on April 19, 1529, against the decree of the Holy Roman Emperor, Charles V, to repeal the concessions that had previously been granted to the followers of Martin Luther (1483–1546), a former Augustinian monk of Erfurt who had been excommunicated for heresy. Except for this purely historical definition, it is hard to give a formula that clearly captures the soul of Protestantism. We have only to cite the two most famous and equally representative Protestant theologians of the twentieth century. According to Karl Barth (1886–1968), Protestantism could be defined by unflinching faithfulness to the Bible. Paul Tillich (1886–1965), on the other hand, defined Protestantism as the refusal of any intermediary between God and the believer.

The sovereign authority of Scripture and salvation by faith in the sole grace of God: these are Protestantism's first principles. Before we go more deeply into these principles and the consequences that were drawn from them, we should note that Protestantism originated as a reforming movement within the Catholic Church, one that at first intended only to purge the Church of real and imagined abuses, and bring her back to her own sources of faith and witness. In truth, Luther and the first generation of Reformers did not think of themselves as ex-Catholics. It is probably the case, for instance, that when Luther's chief aide, Philip Melanchthon, died in 1560 he understood himself to be a Catholic, despite what he viewed as the temporary estrangement from the Roman Church.

In any event, the Protestant Reformation soon developed multiplying internal divisions and had come to reject the principles that had been set down in the beginning; or else these principles were given a sense contrary to traditional Catholicism and to the beliefs and intentions of the first Reformers. Taking the Bible as their sole rule of faith, the most radical of the Reformers, like untrained gardeners in an overgrown garden, hacked about with machetes, slashing unknowingly through elements that had been part and parcel of Christianity for more than a thousand years: sacramental worship, prayers for the dead, Marian doctrine and devotion, fasting, monastic life, clerical celibacy, even the Eucharist. Subsequent generations continued the departure from Catholic faith and practice. By the end of the sixteenth century the older ex-Catholic leadership of former priests, nuns, monks, and friars was replaced by a new leadership that had never celebrated or assisted at Mass, and by a laity that had never confessed its sins to a priest, gone on pilgrimage, prayed the rosary, invoked patron saints, or gained an indulgence. Protestant identity had evolved into something very different from the self-understanding of Luther and his earliest disciples. Unless we understand the Catholic background and context of the early Protestant Reformation, we cannot understand Protestantism.

We therefore set out to examine the causes of the Reformation and the reaction that set in within the Catholic Church to offset the excesses of the Reformers. We must also survey the major Protestant traditions and their denominational embodiments, as well as that amorphous and relatively recent phenomenon called evangelicalism. Our purpose is to show that the Gospel truths professed and lived in these communities can have within the Catholic Church the full flowering that they have never found outside her.

A. *The Reformation: Historical Background*

MARTIN LUTHER'S "REFORMATION BREAKTHROUGH"

October 31, 1517, is a watershed date in Church history. On that day Martin Luther, a priest of the Augustinian order and university professor, posted his Ninety-five Theses on the door of All Saints Cathedral in Wittenberg. His goal was to challenge the selling of indulgences in the traditional fashion of a scholar: he posted his theses, really his grievances, on the church door in hopes of instigating a debate. Little did he know that in a few years he would find himself in the German city of Worms with his life on the line, confronted by the Holy Roman Emperor.

To understand Luther's ideas and why he was willing to die for them, we need historical context. In that vast stretch of time known as the Middle Ages, usually reckoned as A.D. 500–1500, the Catholic Church was the preeminent institution both in the religious and secular realms. Her influence was by no means limited to what was viewed as religious, for European culture as a whole was informed by Christian faith.[189] Church institutions served weary travelers, nursed the sick, and cared for orphans. Almost all schools were Church-run. Monks copied ancient manuscripts and preserved the books of the Bible and much of classical learning for future generations. The Church patronized the arts and music. Because there was no social security, welfare, or unemployment compensation, people in need turned either to their families or to the Church.

As ever, the Church needed money to support her many activities. Churches had to be built, orphanages staffed, and clergy supported. Since most bishops at that time owned manors and received great income from them, a bishopric provided the means to wealth. It was therefore assumed that a donation would be made to the pope when a new bishop was appointed; in fact, bishoprics were often sold to the highest bidder. Simony, the buying or selling of Church offices, was the major vice of the Western Church at that time, despite its repeated condemnation by ecumenical and regional councils, then most recently by Lateran Council IV in 1215. Moreover, when someone became pope, it was assumed by his family members that they should benefit from their relative's good fortune. Thus, all popes saw a steady stream of "nephews" seeking Church jobs. Often they were chosen not for their religious intentions or piety, but for their family connections.

Giovanni de Medici was born at Florence into the wealthiest family of the time. At age fourteen his family purchased for him a cardinal's hat, and in 1513 he was elected pope at the ripe old age of 37, taking the name Leo X. As pope, Leo was conscientious about his religious duties. Although he did not view the papacy as an opportunity to enrich himself, as other popes had, he did wish to beautify Rome and rebuild Saint Peter's Basilica, which was not yet the magnificent church that it now is.

---

[189] As Pope Benedict XVI has asserted, the very idea of Europe was the work of Christian civilization.

To help raise the money for such an undertaking, Leo practically auctioned off the vacant archbishopric of Mainz in Germany, an important position that would generate much revenue for its holder. Albrecht of Brandenburg bid the highest, but he was already the archbishop of Magdeburg, and Church law barred him from holding more than one diocese. Leo agreed to grant Albrecht a dispensation from the rule and to appoint him archbishop of Mainz in return for ten thousand ducats and the first year's income from the archbishopric. Albrecht, for his part, regarded this as an investment and hoped to recoup his expenditure by selling indulgences. Leo authorized the sale of indulgences in the archdiocese for eight years, on condition that half the proceeds go to Rome.

Most Catholics would probably be hard-pressed to explain what, exactly, an indulgence is. To be fair, most Protestants today probably could not articulate the central doctrines of the Reformation. But among those having some knowledge of their religious heritage, there is a vague awareness that Luther's protest began with an attack on indulgences, which had something to do with working or, worse, buying one's way into Heaven.[190] Suffice it to note that indulgences are, and always have been, closely related to Purgatory, which is inexplicable apart from the communion of saints. To recall, the doctrine of Purgatory holds that after death souls not wicked enough to deserve Hell but not yet fit for Heaven must undergo purification before entering Heaven. If, however, the sinner while still on earth confesses his sins with true contrition, does penance, and then gains an indulgence by performing a good work, he can shorten his stay in Purgatory, or perhaps even pass immediately to Heaven. Indulgences may be gained also on behalf of the faithful departed.

Luther's original critique was that the abuses surrounding indulgences—specifically, attaching an indulgence to a financial contribution, which amounted to the sale of indulgences—undercut true penance. Faith, contrition, and discipleship are as important as the good deed, of course, but not all clergymen were clear on that point. Johann Tetzel, the greatest indulgence

---

[190] If you are foggy on indulgences, read the *Catechism of the Catholic Church*, nos. 1471–79.

salesman of his day, is best remembered for his little jingle: "As soon as the coin in the coffer rings / The soul from Purgatory springs." As he roamed the German countryside, the coffer filled many times over, much to the delight of the bishops of Mainz and Rome. Who would be unwilling to spend a few coins to attain salvation?

By the summer of 1518, Luther's case had progressed far enough to require that he present himself in Rome for interrogation. After his territorial ruler, Frederick of Saxony, intervened on his behalf, Luther was summoned instead to Augsburg, where an imperial Diet was in session. Rome acceded to Frederick's wishes, first, because it needed support for a planned crusade against the Ottoman Turks who were poised to invade central Europe from Hungary, and second, because Frederick was one of the electors who would choose the successor of the ailing Holy Roman Emperor Maximilian. The papacy had a vital interest in the outcome of this election.

Things went badly at Augsburg, where for three days in October 1518 Luther met with the pope's representative, Cardinal Cajetan. By this time, what began as a critique of abuses in the practice of indulgences had grown into a dispute over the ultimate question of salvation. Indulgences epitomized for Luther everything that was wrong with the Church: they were human works lacking obvious biblical foundation and abhorrent to the Good News of salvation by grace alone. Luther further asserted the potential fallibility of the papacy and Church councils, particularly in view of the false (to his mind) doctrine of the Church's "treasury." According to this doctrine, set forth by Pope Clement VI in 1343, the source of indulgences is the overflowing "treasury of merits" of Christ and the saints (the latter also being the merits of Christ); this treasury was entrusted to Saint Peter, the key-bearer,[191] and his successors for the benefit of the faithful. The 62nd of Luther's ninety-five theses states: "The true treasury of the Church is the Holy Gospel of the glory and grace of God." Luther challenged Cajetan to refute him from "Scripture and right reason." In Cajetan's view, the debate finally boiled down to papal authority. Having refused to re-

[191] See Matthew 16:19.

cant, Luther returned to Wittenberg, where he continued to lecture and write.

The following month, Leo X issued a bull explaining the doctrine of indulgences and defending the Church's authority to grant them. Luther's views were declared to be in conflict with the Catholic Faith. As Luther saw it, Leo had defined Church teaching without accountability to Scripture, the Fathers of the Church, or the ancient canons. This led Luther eventually to conclude that the Roman Church thought itself above God's revealed Word in the Bible. It was in this context that he came, over the next several years, to believe that the papacy was the prophesied Antichrist of the end times.

Formal proceedings against Luther resumed in the fall of 1519. On June 15, 1520, Leo issued the bull *Exsurge Domine*, which charged that 41 sentences in Luther's various writings were "heretical, scandalous, offensive to pious ears." He gave Luther sixty days to recant and another sixty days to report his recantation to Rome. Luther received the bull on October 10 and defiantly burned it on December 10. The ensuing bull of excommunication, issued on January 3, 1521, formally declared Luther a heretic, as well as his followers and anyone who from then on subscribed to Luther's views.

Ordinarily, those condemned as heretics were arrested by secular authorities and put to death by burning. In Luther's case, however, a complex set of factors made such punishment impossible. The new emperor, Charles V, called for the imperial Diet to meet in the spring at Worms, where Luther should be given a formal hearing. Although Charles guaranteed Luther's safety, it would nonetheless be risky for the German friar to leave Wittenberg, for nearly a century earlier the Bohemian priest Jan Hus was burned at the stake after being summoned to the Council of Constance on an imperial pledge of safe conduct. Even so, Luther appeared before the Diet at Worms on April 17, 1521. According to a traditional but apocryphal account, on the following day, when urged to disavow his writings, he replied, "Here I stand. I can do no other. God help me. Amen."

Luther then took part in intense discussions involving the papal legate, Elector Frederick, and representatives of the Emperor. Despite every effort to induce him to recant, Luther repudiated not a single sentence from the forty-one cited in Leo's bull. On April 26, he hastily left Worms. While headed for Wittenberg he was whisked away to safety by Frederick's soldiers and spent a year in hiding at the fortified castle at Wartburg, where he began work on one of his foremost achievements, the translation of the New Testament into German—although his was not the first German translation. At the conclusion of the Diet at Worms a month later, he was put under the imperial ban and his books were ordered destroyed.

In March 1522, after almost a year in seclusion at Wartburg, Luther returned to Wittenberg, bereft of the power to act at Church or state level but with many supporters. The rupture between Rome and the budding Reformation was complete. Now, all the energy of Luther's theological vision was harnessed to the forces already at work to dissolve the Church's unity.

But how did Luther's original criticism of indulgence sales become entangled with a controversy over the sources of authority in the Church, a controversy that resulted in the fracturing of western Christendom and more than a century of religious warfare? The answer is bound up with Luther's spiritual and psychological grappling.

We will never know precisely what happened to Luther in the years between his becoming an Augustinian monk in 1505 and his dramatic attack on indulgences in 1517. But we know from his contemporary lecture notes and from his later writings that he underwent years of harrowing emotional and intellectual tension, which finally resulted in a "conversion" experience probably in the year 1513. The nature of this experience shaped the main features of Protestant belief and the direction taken by the Reformation. It is important, therefore—difficult as it is—to sketch the German friar's inner struggles and their outcome.

Luther was one of the most pious and diligent monks at Erfurt. "If ever a monk got to Heaven by his monkery," he would later write, "I certainly should have got there." [192] Yet he was haunted from the start by doubts about whether he, a sinner, could ever stand approved before the all-holy God. He spent many sleepless

---

[192] Luther, *A Short Answer to Duke George's Latest Book* (1533). Quoted in James MacKinnon, *Luther and the Reformation*, vol. 1, *Early Life and Religious Development to 1517* (London: Longmans, Green & Co., 1925), p. 93.

nights in prayer, constantly confessed his sins, fasted sometimes three days without a crumb, scourged his body, and still could gain no sense of being forgiven.

The cause of Luther's turmoil has been, and will ever be, a matter of conjecture. Perhaps his notion of God as a stern Judge had something to do with the character of his father, a hard-working copper miner, devoted to his family but strict and fiery-tempered. Luther had vowed to become a monk in a moment of panic during a thunderstorm, seeing in the monastic state the most effective means to holiness. The fact that he immediately regretted it but went through with it (against his father's will) might have contributed to his later tension. What is quite certain is that the Nominalist theology in which Luther had been educated strongly emphasized what were called "good works," a term which included pious practices such as doing penance, fasting, going on a pilgrimage, gaining an indulgence, as well as acts of charity—and in all this, salvation seemed the work of man merely crowned or completed by God.

Luther was high-strung, with keen sensibilities and a sensitive conscience, not the kind to persuade himself easily that he was doing the best he could and that the rest should be left to God, as his spiritual advisers urged. Nor did his journey to Rome in the autumn of 1510 bring him relief. Already on the verge of despair, he was appalled and disillusioned at the iniquity he witnessed in the heart of western Christendom among the general population and all ranks of the clergy.

The following year, Luther was called from the cloister to a professorship at the University of Wittenberg, where he immersed himself in the study of Scripture. In what might be called the standard Protestant account, Luther's reading and the influence of his friends began to suggest a remedy for his spiritual anguish. As he recounted many years later, something happened while reading Saint Paul's Letter to the Romans:

> I saw the inner connection between the two phrases, "The justice of God is revealed in the Gospel" and "The just shall live by faith". I began to understand that this "justice of God" is the righteousness by which the just man lives through the free gift of God, that is to say "by faith." ...

Thereupon I felt as if I had been born again and had entered Paradise through wide-open gates. Immediately the whole of Scripture took on a new meaning for me.[193]

Now all Luther's previous ideas were reversed: salvation is a grace, a gift of God, not the work of man. What we could not do, God in His Son has done for us. One is saved not by good works but by faith in the utterly gratuitous love of God in Christ. This faith is itself God's gift to undeserving sinners.

At this point it must be said that Catholicism had never officially taught otherwise. In fact, Church councils had condemned the false idea of salvation that vexed Luther for so long and that he came to oppose. But circumstances had blinded Luther to those parts of Scripture and Tradition favorable to his new insight. He had been schooled in quite other than the theology of Saint Thomas Aquinas, who at the height of the Middle Ages had systematized the traditional teaching on the respective roles of God and man in the work of salvation.

Between 1520, when Luther wrote the tracts that are still the best expression of his ideas, and 1530, when the chief tenets of the Lutheran Church were summarized in the Augsburg Confession of Faith, the main lines of Protestant belief were worked out by Luther and his colleagues in Wittenberg, with some contributions from independent leaders of revolt against Rome. In particular, Luther and those first Reformers offered relatively new answers to questions that go far back in Christian history. To the question how is a person to be saved, they answered: Not by works but by faith. To the question "Where does religious authority lie?" they answered: Not in the visible institution known as the Church of Rome but in Holy Scripture. Salvation by grace alone received through faith alone, and the supreme authority of the Bible: these two principles are the starting point of the Reformation and the bedrock of Protestantism. As we shall observe, the individualistic and erroneous conclusions the Reformers drew from these principles brought about not only their separation from the Catholic Church but also internal divisions within Protestantism.

[193] Preface to the 1545 edition of Luther's Collected Works. Quoted in E. Harris Harbison, *The Age of Reformation* (Ithaca, N.Y.: Cornell University Press, 1955), p. 49.

Harvard historian Steven Ozment describes the startling transformation a visitor to a Protestant city would perceive just a decade or two after Luther's revolt: the churches stripped and whitewashed, the monasteries and convents closed except for a few cloisters housing elderly religious who could not be pensioned off, the remaining clergy married, the Holy Sacrifice of the Mass replaced by a Communion service.[194] What began as a reforming movement within the Catholic Church became a frontal assault on contemporary Catholicism, which in Luther's mind and in Protestant propaganda was a perversion of Christianity amounting to a false Church. How did this come to be?

As we saw, Luther's basic insight was that man is justified, or accepted by God, not by his own moral effort but only by God's grace received through faith in Jesus Christ. On its face, this view of salvation was neither heretical nor novel. A thousand years earlier Saint Augustine, the "Doctor of Grace," had stressed man's impotence before God.[195] But Luther and his disciples made "justification by faith" the sum and substance of Christianity, the one criterion by which everything in the Church was to be judged, as if Christian faith and devotion consists solely of the sin/grace antithesis. But what about the Incarnation, our supernatural adoption, the future restoration of all things in Christ, human divinization through grace, or our adherence to Christ for His own sake?

Not only that, the principles of *sola gratia* (grace alone) and *sola fides* (faith alone)—two sides of the same coin—were understood as requiring certain departures from Catholic Tradition. In Luther's perception, the Mass and all other devotions were "works." Baptism and the Eucharist were the only two sacraments with strong biblical warrant, although in the *Babylonian Captivity of the Church* (1520) Luther endorsed private confession as "useful and necessary" for distressed souls. The dead were not to be prayed for because they were either already instantly beatified by faith alone, or hopelessly damned for lack of it. Protestant theology attributed no special powers to priests and obliterated any real distinction between the clergy and laity.

---

[194] Steven Ozment, *Protestants: The Birth of a Revolution* (New York: Doubleday, 1992), at pp. 26–28.

[195] See, for example, Augustine's treatise *On Nature and Grace* (written A.D. 415).

No longer was there any rationale for monasticism or religious vows. At Wittenberg, Luther's friary became his family home as he married off the local nuns and eventually took as his wife a former nun, Katherine von Bora, who bore him six children.

Catholic theologians naturally reacted to assert those truths that the Reformation had denied or neglected. And so, when Protestants declared that salvation is entirely God's doing, understood as if any effort on our part were useless, Catholics answered that grace enables human cooperation in the process of salvation. By the same token, when Protestants asserted that salvation is obtained through faith in terms that boil down to denying the importance of good works, Catholics answered that true faith produces good works. When Protestants asserted that every Christian shares in Christ's unique priesthood and is therefore gifted for a ministry of some kind, Catholics responded that Christ conferred on the Apostles a priesthood distinct, in essence and function, from that of God's people as a whole. And when Protestants set the Bible over against the Church, and in particular against those elements of Tradition not explicitly attested in Scripture, Catholics defended the authority of popes, councils, and creeds, not in opposition to Scripture, but in order to prevent its true sense from being distorted.

But counterbalances came too late to avert the greatest schism in Christendom since 1054. By the time of Luther's death in 1546, Germany was already divided between Lutheran and Catholic states and was on the verge of religious warfare. Scandinavia and England had left the Catholic fold—though England, as we shall see, was unique in its Reformation—and Protestant doctrines were gaining acceptance in the Netherlands, France, and elsewhere. It was not long into the century when the Reformers discovered that they had, in Ozment's words, "sown the wind."[196] Once the initial break with Rome occurred, there was no stopping the proliferation of Protestant sects, some far more radical than Luther ever could have imagined.

In Switzerland, Ulrich Zwingli (1484–1531), a secular priest, led a partly independent reform at Zurich. Like Luther, Zwingli

[196] Ozment, *Protestants*, p. 217.

believed that the Mass was not a sacrifice. But the two men disagreed on whether Christ is truly present in the Eucharist. Although Luther rejected the doctrine of transubstantiation as unbiblical and irrational, he insisted that the elements of bread and wine are *sacramental* signs of Christ's Body and Blood, meaning that they contain and communicate what they signify. Zwingli, by contrast, repeatedly quoted Jesus' statement that "the flesh profits nothing," [197] and insisted that the Lord's Supper was not a literal eating and drinking of Christ. This was the first of many divisions within Protestantism. Since Zwingli felt less reverence for the past than Luther, the change of appearance and worship in Swiss churches was more revolutionary than in the Lutheran churches of Germany. Zwinglian ministers faced the congregation in prayer, wore lay clothes, and distributed bread and wine from a table in the middle of the nave. Lutheran ministers, initially at least, continued to face the altar, elevate the host, and wear Mass vestments.

Luther and Zwingli represent the first phase of the Protestant movement. John Calvin (1509–1564), a Frenchman at Geneva, represents the second. We will soon get acquainted with Calvin's "Reformed" Protestantism, a name which first came into common use when opposed, not to the Catholics, but to the Lutherans. The Reformation turned its adherents into permanent revolutionaries.

JOHN CALVIN AND "REFORMED" PROTESTANTISM

The second generation of Protestant Reformers felt the need for a systematic theology and a disciplined Church organization, and it was Jehan Cauvin, whom the English-speaking world remembers as John Calvin, who supplied them. Calvin was born in 1509 at Noyon, northeast of Paris, and educated as a humanist and lawyer. By his mid-twenties he appears to have accepted the Reformation agenda. On a chance visit to the Swiss merchant city of Geneva in 1536 he met the local Protestant leader, William Farel, who invited him to put aside his career plans and help consolidate the Reformation in that city. Except for three years of exile (1538–1541), Calvin remained in Geneva as the

---

[197] John 6:63.

city's leading minister and unofficial "city manager" until his death.

What Saint Thomas Aquinas had done for medieval Catholicism in systematizing doctrine, Calvin had done for Protestantism. His *Institutes of the Christian Religion* (first edition 1536, final edition 1559) was the definitive theological treatise of all Protestantism and is widely regarded as the most significant religious work of the sixteenth century. It went through edition after edition in almost every major European language and influenced the thought of generations of Protestants in Europe and North America.

Calvin's brand of Protestantism was no mere variant of Lutheranism. Whereas Luther regarded justification by faith as the nucleus of all Christian doctrines, Calvin's central belief around which all else revolved was the absolute sovereignty of God and, as a consequence of that, the predestination of man. God, said Calvin, is "the Arbiter and Governor of all things, Who, in His own wisdom, has, from the remotest eternity, decreed what He would do, and now, by His own power, executes what He has decreed." It follows that God "has once and for all determined both whom He would admit to salvation, and whom He would condemn to destruction." Those predestined to eternal life are the "elect," and their salvation is a given even before they come to faith: this is to show forth the utter gratuitousness of God's mercy. The rest are destined for eternal punishment, and were born into this world for that very purpose: this is to show forth God's justice in judging sin. If this seems unjust by human standards, we must remember that "the will of God is the highest rule of justice, so that what He wills must be considered just, for this very reason, because He wills it." [198]

As an account of human life this is hideous, but we must not suppose that Calvin spun it from thin air. Had not Luther, Saint Augustine, and Saint Paul all insisted that we are saved solely by grace received through faith? And was it not established doctrine that even faith itself is a gift of God? Since some people come to faith and others do not, it would seem that from eternity God elects some to salvation and rejects others to damnation. Calvin

[198] John Calvin, *Institutes* I, 16, 8; III, 21, 7; III, 23, 2.

was convinced that this was the Apostle's teaching in Romans 9:6–24. Moreover, it was not Calvin but Augustine who first discussed predestination in all its implications. As a consequence of original sin, Augustine theorized, God has justly predestined the overwhelming majority of people to eternal punishment, but has graciously predestined some to eternal life. (This belief was widely accepted in the West, though it has spawned many heresies and controversies.) On the face of it, Calvin stands squarely in the Augustinian tradition, especially on the Catholic understanding of grace. For him, as for Augustine, divine election was the final proof that everything is of grace, including the division between those who accept the Good News and those who reject it.

But Calvin passed beyond Augustine, who held that none can know for certain whether or not he is elect. By contrast, Calvin regarded the doctrine of predestination as the indestructible foundation for the Christian assurance of salvation: "We shall never be properly convinced that the source of our salvation is the gratuitous mercy of God," said Calvin, "until His eternal election becomes known to us; for this puts in a clear light the grace of God, showing He does not admit all and sundry to the grace of salvation, but contrasts His gift to some with its denial to others." [199] On this point Catholics and Calvinists took opposing sides at the time of the Reformation.

Calvin differed from Augustine also in considering predestination independently of original sin. God, for His own glorification and without any regard to Adam's sin, has created some as "vessels of mercy" destined for glory and others as "vessels of wrath" destined for doom. At no time did Calvin grant that Adam's fall was due to his own free will. Those created for Hell God also predestined for sin, and whatever faith and holiness they may exhibit are only apparent, for grace is efficacious only in those predestined for Heaven. Thus Calvin could declare plainly that Christ died not for all mankind but only for the elect. All the important questions were settled long ago, and human planning is, in any case, *une chiquenaude de Dieu*—the flick of God's middle finger. Why should we ponder, when it is not we

---

[199] *Institutes* III, 21, 7

who decide? Why should we labor, when it is not we who accomplish?

Was Calvin's cast-iron logic the true interpretation of the New Testament and the Catholic Tradition? For the next hundred years this was the key question for theologians, for the Catholics almost as much as for the Protestants.

Recall that Calvin got much of his Calvinism from Saint Augustine, although his theory of predestination differed from Augustine's on some points. To Calvin, God's eternal decrees were absolute, that is, not in any way regardful of man's good or evil choices. God stands to us in the relation of a playwright to his play: the characters say and do whatever he makes them say and do. Our first parents, like ourselves, could not have avoided sinning, because God decreed Adam's fall as the means to an end, namely, God's selection of some for everlasting life while leaving the others to their decreed doom. Following this line of thought, Calvin reasoned that Christ died not for sinners—that is, for every last one of us—but only for the elect.

The Catholic Church accepts as a revealed truth the predestination of the elect to eternal life, but also affirms free will, thus staking out a position distinct from Calvinism. Adam need not have sinned, neither was his fall from grace preordained. Christ died for the whole human race; therefore the damned could never blame God for their ruin, for God only permitted it, without positively desiring it. God desires to save all, and so He denies the necessary grace to none, though some, perhaps many, will reject grace.

Calvin matched the intellectual achievement of his *Institutes* with a working model of a church and community, which by the year 1600 was replicated as far to the east as Hungary. From all over Europe, young Protestant enthusiasts went to Geneva to see what the Scottish reformer John Knox described as "the most perfect school of Christ that ever was on earth since the days of the apostles." [200]

Calvin's Geneva was in fact a puritanical theocracy. Church attendance was enforced under pain of severe punishment. Taverns were abolished, and in the cafés set up in their stead, strin-

---

[200] Harbison, *The Age of Reformation*, p. 77.

gent regulations banned bawdy songs. Innkeepers had to ensure their customers said grace before meals. To smile during a church service or sleep during a sermon was to risk imprisonment. It was forbidden to play dice, sing a secular song, or give a child a non-biblical name. Dancing, skating, and card playing were likewise prohibited. Every offense, even the most paltry, was carefully entered in the records of the Consistory. Between 1542 and 1546 there were 58 executions, among them the beheading of a child for striking its parents.

For fear of undercutting Christ's atoning sacrifice on the Cross, Luther and all subsequent Protestants denied the sacrificial nature of the Eucharist and even went so far as to call the Mass idolatrous and abominable. Still, unlike Zwingli and Calvin, Luther at least retained belief in a real objective presence of Christ in the Eucharist. Calvin argued that because Christ's glorified body is in Heaven, it could not be on earth; thus what is received in the Lord's Supper is but a symbol. To Catholics and Lutherans alike, this was heresy. And so, neither Calvinist nor Catholic worship was tolerated in Lutheran states, while Calvinists, for their part, punished anyone found holding either the Catholic or Lutheran understanding of the Real Presence.

Calvin went further than Luther or Zwingli in banishing the trappings of the Catholic liturgy. Calvinist churches were houses of preaching, where the pulpit had abolished the altar. True piety, said Calvin, is preserved only by inward obedience to God's Word, the Bible. Images and statues, incense, the organ, hymns (except the Psalms), vestments, candles—anything that could interest the senses was cast aside. Even the church bells remained silent in Geneva, for the true believer need not be reminded of his duty by the clang of metal. With one stroke Calvin erased saints' days and feast-days from the calendar, including Easter and Christmas.

The international Reformed churches inspired by Calvin maintained the principle of congregational election in choosing the orders of ministers, teachers, presbyters (elders), and deacons. An important share in Church government was accorded the laity, but in practice the clergy exercised a strong control over their congregations in matters of belief and conduct. None were allowed in the pulpit unless publicly called, and ordination, which Calvin regarded almost as a sacrament, was conferred by the presbyters.

While bitterly anti-papal, Calvin was also fearful of the threat of anarchy from various groups on the Reformation's "left wing." These were the Radical Reformers who felt that official Protestantism—Lutheran, Zwinglian, Calvinist—was little better than medieval Catholicism. For in spite of all the talk about justification by faith alone, the Bible as the sole rule of faith, and the priesthood of all Christians, the established Protestant churches retained an ordained clergy who baptized infants and, in the case of the Lutherans, administered Communion with reverence for the Real Presence.

These radicals were generally called "Anabaptists," meaning persons who believed in "rebaptism," which had been declared a heresy punishable by death ten centuries before.[201] But they called themselves simply "Baptists," meaning that they thought infant Baptism unscriptural and thus no sacrament at all. The true Church, they insisted, is a voluntary association of disciples who have experienced spiritual rebirth, have been baptized into membership—as the early Christians were—as adults, and now live godly lives in obedience to the Scriptures. A strict sort of democracy applied within Anabaptist churches, as each community elected its own pastor.

Fearing social and religious revolution from below, Luther and Calvin fought a brutal two-front war against the Catholics on the right and the Anabaptists on the left. From these internal divisions within the Reformation emerged the major families of Protestantism.

THE REFORMATION IN ENGLAND

One of the peculiar elements of the Reformation in England was that the breach with the papacy had preceded rather than followed doctrinal dispute. King Henry VIII's (reigned 1509–1547) desire to obtain an annulment of his marriage to Catherine of Aragon (his brother Arthur's widow) because he needed a male heir to the throne and because he wanted to marry Anne Boleyn (one of Catherine's ladies in waiting) was the direct cause of

---

[201] Code of Justinian (A.D. 529).

England's departure from the Catholic Church. In 1527 Catherine was past childbearing. The lack of a male heir might throw England into war, and Henry was infatuated with Anne. Catherine was the aunt of the Holy Roman Emperor Charles V, and Pope Clement VII was under the emperor's thumb. It was not surprising, therefore, that the Pope should deny the King's wish, regardless of the strength or weakness of Henry's case.

When tact and persuasion failed, Henry resorted to threats. Cardinal Wolsey, Lord Chancellor of England, failed to procure the annulment, so Henry dismissed and arrested him. Wolsey escaped execution by dying first. His replacement, Thomas Cromwell, worked to mobilize the whole nation in Henry's support in order to threaten the Pope with schism unless the annulment were granted. In 1531 the English clergy, assembled in Convocation, were intimidated into acknowledging Henry as "Supreme Head of the Church in England," and next year they gave up their right to make laws for the Church apart from the King and Parliament.

In the spring of 1533, Anne was pregnant and the pace was quickened. Threats gave way to acts. Parliament passed a statute cutting off appeals from English ecclesiastical courts to Rome, and the new Archbishop of Canterbury, Thomas Cranmer, straightaway held court and granted Henry his annulment, enabling him to make Anne his queen. In 1534 a series of acts of Parliament finally stopped all financial payments and judicial appeals to Rome, declared that "the King's Majesty justly and rightfully is and ought to be . . . the only Supreme Head in earth of the Church of England," and fixed the succession to the throne upon the children of Henry and Anne (their only child, Elizabeth, was born in September 1533). Within the next few years some 550 English monasteries were dissolved, their property confiscated by the crown, and their seven thousand monks and nuns pensioned and thrust out into secular life. Henry had cut England off from the Church of Rome.

All this amounted to a revolution. In medieval England, as in the rest of Christendom, Church and State worked hand in glove, no matter how confusing the conflicts and compromises between the two powers. Spiritual jurisdiction belonged to the clergy, temporal jurisdiction to the king and his representatives. It was hard to draw the line in practice, but in theory there was a clear delineation. Now the king was "Supreme Head" of the Church in England. What did this mean? Had the State absorbed the Church? Had Henry stepped into the "shoes of the fisherman" so far as one nation was concerned, without of course claiming the priestly power to celebrate Mass and absolve sins? The answer was a tentative yes, but no clear answer ever was given. The closest approach was the famous preamble to the Act in Restraint of Appeals of 1533, which put forth this theory: England was a sovereign nation subject to a single monarch; within this nation clergy and laity alike were subjects owing obedience to the king; no foreign prince, including the Bishop of Rome, had any jurisdiction whatever in England.

And yet this theory left all the important questions unanswered. What, then, is the "Catholic Church"? Where is the ultimate authority in the Church? Did this mean that England had joined the Lutheran fold? No, Henry insisted. In doctrine and worship, the Church of England was still very much Catholic, and an "Act Abolishing Diversity of Opinions" was put through Parliament in 1539 to stress this fact by reaffirming the Real Presence of Christ in the Eucharist and other points of orthodox belief. But a significant phrase in the Act of Supremacy of 1534, repeated in other legislation, gave the king "full power and authority . . . to visit, repress, redress, reform, order, correct, restrain, and amend all . . . errors, heresies, abuses, offenses . . . whatsoever they be," in the English Church. This was, in effect, the most spectacular response to Luther's appeal to secular rulers to take in hand the matter of Church reform because the clergy had failed to reform themselves. What happened in England under Henry VIII was the establishment of the legal supremacy of the State over the Church—indeed, the establishment of a national Church.

The revolt was accomplished with relatively little bloodshed, the martyrdoms, in 1535, of Sir Thomas More and Bishop John Fisher being the best known of the executions.[202] The average churchgoer saw no significant change in doctrine or worship. The net result was that Englishmen at first generally accepted the

---

[202] Robert Bolt's impressive play and movie script for *A Man for All Seasons* brings clarity to Saint Thomas More the man and has much to teach us about Peter's principle: "We must obey God rather than men" (Acts 5:29).

break with Rome without effective protest, although there is no evidence that the majority wanted it.

Henry had separated the *Ecclesia Anglicana* from the Church of Rome with an ideology skillfully devised so that his subjects might feel they were in substantial continuity with the Church they had always known. The one profound change had been the substitution of the King's supremacy for the Pope's. Otherwise little was altered: the Mass was still a sacrifice, the sacraments retained their supernatural efficacy, the bishops remained the successors of the Apostles, and the Blessed Virgin was no less revered. If there was one noticeable difference at the time, it was that English Bibles were placed in all the churches. Now people were reading God's Word and what came out of Wittenberg, Zurich, and other hotbeds of the Reformation. Archbishop Cranmer led a small but determined Protestant-minded party. England at the time of Henry's death was headed in the direction of more extreme Protestantism.

The eleven years between Henry's death in 1547 and the accession of Queen Elizabeth in 1558 saw violent swings of the religious pendulum under Elizabeth's younger half-brother Edward VI (reigned 1547–1553) and her older half-sister Mary Tudor (reigned 1553–1558). Under the boy-king Edward, the Protestant party gained control of the government and swung England more clearly into the Protestant camp. It was a strange and confused six years in which Archbishop Cranmer gave his countrymen *The Book of Common Prayer* (1549), that masterpiece of English style and religious compromise, which follows the basic outline of the medieval Mass but at crucial points inculcates Protestant heresies. Cranmer himself soon found it too Catholic, and in 1552 revised it to simplify the liturgy along Calvinist lines: all allusion to altar or sacrifice was studiously expunged.

Meanwhile, some of the most unscrupulous adventurers in English history were scheming to exclude Mary Tudor, the Catholic daughter of Henry's first queen, Catherine of Aragon, from the throne in favor of their puppet, Lady Jane Grey. Since there was no popular demand for "reformation" in England in the years prior to Henry's break with Rome, most of the English people were glad to see Mary make good her claim to the throne in 1553. Everyone knew that Mary would return England to the

Catholic fold. An Act of Parliament restored the papal supremacy in England (1554–1555). A few monasteries were reestablished, Westminster Abbey being the most important.

But Mary made two big political mistakes. First, she married Philip II of Spain, in spite of the patriotic protests of her council, her parliament, and her people. Second, she permitted the execution of about 300 persons for Protestant heresy, most of them obscure, ordinary folk except for Cranmer and his associates. Deservedly or not, Spain and Catholic fanaticism became indissolubly associated in the English mind, and the Protestantism that Cranmer could not sell to the majority of Englishmen when he was in power became the mark of an English patriot. "The reigns of Edward VI and Mary had made the Catholics more Roman and the Protestants more Reformed," writes Cambridge historian Owen Chadwick.[203]

As the daughter of Henry VIII and Anne Boleyn, Elizabeth (reigned 1558–1603) had no choice but to espouse the Protestant cause, though in the interests of national unity she had to move cautiously. The Elizabethan Settlement reflected a policy of expediency in religious matters. Papal jurisdiction in England was once more rejected, yet the young queen shrank from assuming the title of "Supreme Head" of the Church, taking instead the title "Supreme Governor." Like her father, she claimed no powers of ministry but reasserted Henry's claim that in ecclesiastical matters the Crown always has the last word. Cranmer's Prayer Book, revised again in 1559, was once more made the basis of public worship, and *Thirty-Nine Articles of Religion* (1563) were drawn up, both documents reflecting strong Protestant influence.

The Elizabethan Settlement laid the basis for what is today called Anglicanism. The Anglican ideal, never quite put into words, was a broad national religion that would blend the Catholic and Protestant elements in a way that would unify as many Englishmen as possible in one Church. In this way, the Church of England came to include both the followers of continental Protestantism, especially in its Calvinist form, and those who remained attached to the "Old Religion," as Catholicism

---

[203] Owen Chadwick, *The Penguin History of the Church*, vol. 3, *The Reformation* (1964; New York: Penguin Books, 1990), p. 131.

was then called. Queen Elizabeth turned a deaf ear to the "Puritan" Calvinists who hoped to rid the national Church of every last vestige of Catholicism and replace the office of bishop with a presbyterian form of government. Consequently, the Calvinists never succeeded in dominating the Church of England the way they did the Scottish and Dutch churches, even though they played an important, if belated, role in English Protestantism. Both in England and on the European continent, Calvinists eventually split into a host of separate sects that often bickered among themselves. Some of Calvinism's key doctrines were abandoned, and few Protestants today profess Calvinism whole and undiluted.

The English Reformation was substantially a part of the Protestant Reformation, although it was lust, not dogma, that set in motion England's departure from the Catholic Church. Just three years after Cranmer pronounced Henry and Catherine not married and Henry and Anne married, he found himself pronouncing Henry and Anne not married: this was to make room for Jane Seymour, the third of Henry's six wives. Anne was beheaded on trumped up charges of adultery, incest, and treason.

Henry's marital history bears some analogy to the history of the Church in general and the Reformation in particular. Just as Henry regarded each new wife as his "true" love and rationalized each new marriage as a divinely sanctioned righting of wrongs (the fault lying always with his previous wife), so the history of Christianity is littered with "reformers" who have reestablished the "true Church," usually in opposition to the allegedly false Church of Rome, and then, later, in opposition to their own previously true churches.

SUMMARY

The four major movements of the Protestant Reformation—Lutheran, Reformed (Calvinist), Radical (Anabaptist), and Anglican—all center on Luther's key principles of *sola gratia* (salvation by grace alone) and *sola scriptura* (Scripture alone as the source and authority for doctrine). Especially useful to our present purpose is the work of Father Louis Bouyer (1913–2004), a Lutheran convert to Catholic Church. In his book *The Spirit and Forms of Protestantism*, Bouyer argues that the Reformation *solas* were essentially consistent with Catholic belief, but that Luther and the Reformers had drawn erroneous conclusions from them.

Luther's basic intuition, that without grace man can neither dispose himself for salvation nor attain it, is perfectly orthodox. The Council of Trent reiterated the teaching of the Second Council of Orange (529), which asserted that human free will is so weakened as a result of original sin that we cannot love God and neighbor as we ought unless moved by grace. Nevertheless, Trent added, we freely cooperate in our own salvation, yet our cooperation is itself the fruit of grace. (Precisely how this is so is a mystery, and the Church was careful not to commit herself to any particular theological explanation.) Therefore, Bouyer concludes, "the Catholic not only may, but must, in virtue of his own faith, give a full and unreserved adherence to the *sola gratia*, understood in the positive sense we have seen upheld by Protestants." [204]

But what about the flipside of *sola gratia*, the Protestant claim that the grace of justification is received *sola fide*, through faith *alone*? The answer depends on what "faith" means. Catholic theologians in the late Middle Ages generally defined faith as a grace-enabled intellectual assent to the truths of revelation: God gives us faith so that we can entrust ourselves to Him in hope and love. Faith, in this sense, is but the beginning of salvation; without charity, also the work of grace, it is not "saving faith" but dead faith. [205] The Reformers, on the other hand, spoke of faith as a trusting response to what God has done for us in Christ. Doing the right thing for the wrong reason, they rejected the Catholic "faith *and* good works" because they misunderstood it to mean that God does His part, and man in turn does his part independently of grace. Catholics can accept *sola fide* if care is taken not to oppose faith to charity.

Before we turn to the principle of *sola scriptura*, another clarification is in order. The farther Luther advanced in his conflicts with Rome, the more closely he identified *sola gratia* with a particular theory known as forensic justification, that is, justification

---

[204] Louis Bouyer, *The Spirit and Forms of Protestantism* (1956; repr. Princeton, N.J.: Scepter Publishers, 2001), p. 72.

[205] See James 2:20.

as a legal declaration. According to this view, we sinners can stand innocent before God's tribunal because God acquits us by a kind of legal fiction, crediting to us the absolute holiness of Christ even while we continue to stay stuck in the mire of sin. In Luther's words, the Christian is *simul iustus et peccator*, at once justified and a sinner. By contrast, the common teaching of the Church prior to the Reformation holds that God justifies sinners, not merely by declaring them righteous on account of Christ's sacrifice, but by transforming them interiorly, removing all that can properly be called sin and establishing His grace within them.

Turning now to the matter of Scripture, no serious Christian would dispute that God's Word, rather than man's, must govern the life of the Church. Since the canonical Scriptures alone have God as their primary Author, the Bible possesses a unique authority: this, says Bouyer, is the sense in which Catholics can accept *sola scriptura*. At the same time, the sovereign authority of Scripture does not imply that God's Word should be interpreted apart from the Church's creeds, councils, liturgy, and moral codes. The Church is "the pillar and bulwark of the truth." [206] To her the Apostles entrusted what they had received from the Lord,[207] namely, the revealed truths certified in Scripture and the early creeds. Indeed, the Tradition and authority of the Church were needed to determine which books did or did not belong in the Bible. In the Catholic view, Scripture and Tradition form an indissoluble whole that is authoritatively interpreted by the successors of the Apostles.

The problem arose, Bouyer informs us, when many Protestants took the position that Scripture alone conveyed God's Word, and was therefore the norm by which all doctrines and practices were to be tested. They did so, not in opposition to Catholicism initially, but to the Radicals "who declined to accept any authority other than themselves." [208] Just the same, the links between the Bible and the Church were severed, and Scripture came to be seen, paradoxically, as alien to the very Tradition that had produced it and handed it down over the centuries. Having

---

[206] 1 Timothy 3:15.
[207] See 1 Corinthians 11:23; 15:3.
[208] Bouyer, *The Spirit and Forms of Protestantism*, p. 144.

wrenched Scripture from the rule of faith and its authoritative teachers, the Reformers unwittingly undercut the truth of *sola scriptura*: now the Bible's authority extended only so far as the individual believer's interpretation of it allowed.

As paradoxical as it may seem, all of this suggests, first, that it is possible to reinterpret the most substantial Protestant principles in a sense that is no longer basically anti-Catholic, and second, that those principles are best safeguarded within the full stream of Tradition that is Catholicism.

B. *Contemporary Protestantism*

Now that we have considered the immediate causes, distinctive doctrines, and early splintering of the Protestant Reformation, we are ready to traverse the landscape of contemporary Protestantism, examining in turn each of its chief branches and their denominational offshoots. But before we begin exploring the worlds within the world of Protestantism, it is useful to note some of the characteristics of present-day Protestantism, taken as a whole.

It is not an insult but a simple observation that Protestantism has never achieved the unity of a single Church. Such unity, in any meaningful sense of the word, is absolutely excluded by the Reformation principle of "Scripture alone," inasmuch as this is taken to mean Scripture divorced from the authoritative Tradition of the community of faith, past and present. Following Luther's break with Rome, *sola scriptura* quickly devolved into the principle of private interpretation of Scripture: each one is free to decide for himself what constitutes true, "biblical" Christianity. To be fair, there are Protestants who hold, as Catholics do, that individual ideas of what the Bible means must be liable to discussion and assessment by the wider fellowship. But because there is not in Protestantism a Magisterium comparable to that of the Catholic Church, and because no Protestant communion even claims to be *the* Church of Christ, any attempt to decide a doctrinal controversy, determine a point of liturgy, or enact a single detail of church discipline results in further division, such that the differences among Protestants are often as great and as basic as their differences with Catholics.

Some examples are illustrative. Although the Protestant churches generally recognize two sacraments only—Baptism and the Eucharist (or "Lord's Supper")—they are divided over whether these function as channels of grace or mere symbols of grace; those which take the latter view prefer to speak of "ordinances" rather than "sacraments." Some churches practice infant Baptism, while others reject it as unscriptural. Some come close to a Catholic understanding of the Eucharist; others reject the concept of the Real Presence. These differences are found not only among members of the different denominations, but also among the members of the same denomination. Anglicanism, which regards itself as a *via media* between Protestantism and Catholicism, contains three distinct and competing parties: the "High Church" party accepts virtually every doctrine of Catholicism except the primacy and infallibility of the pope; the "Low Church" is thoroughly Protestant in its teachings and practices; the "Broad Church" is rationalistic and makes no definite statement of doctrine.

In trying to sort out the bewildering varieties of Protestantism, it is somewhat helpful to classify the denominations according to their form of church governance, or polity. Some are congregational, others are presbyterian, and still others are episcopal. Each of these polities is defended as representing that of the Church in apostolic times.

In a congregational polity, each local congregation is autonomous and operates through democratic processes. It hires and fires its ministers, elects its own officers, holds title to all property, and perhaps formulates its own statement of faith. Denominations that are congregational in polity, besides the Congregationalists themselves, are the Baptists, Disciples of Christ, the United Church of Christ, and many Holiness and Pentecostal groups.

Churches organized with a presbyterian polity are governed by a group of elected elders, or "presbyters" (from the Greek *presbyteros,* elder), and in most cases espouse either classic or modified Calvinism. The larger church supervises the individual congregations through presbyteries or associations of churches in a given area. Clerical and lay presbyters cast equal votes, and no individual holds an ecclesiastical office superior to another. In addition to the uppercase Presbyterians, the various Reformed Churches of Europe are presbyterian in polity.

The episcopal polity, which is that of the Catholic and Orthodox Churches, is hierarchical in structure, with the chief authority over the local Church (a diocese or its equivalent) resting in a bishop (Greek *episkopos*, overseer). The clergy who serve within the local Church depend on the bishop for the legitimate exercise of their ministry. Anglicanism and its American branch, the Episcopal Church, as well as most Lutheran and Methodist churches, maintain an episcopal polity, although in most cases the bishops are elected rather than appointed as in the Catholic Church.

Viewing Protestant Christianity from the perspective of church organization is only partially useful, however. Some newer Presbyterian communities have an episcopal type of constitution, with the office of bishop, and appointed consistories instead of elected synods, while some Baptist churches are moving away from a congregational polity toward presbyterian models. In this and other respects, denominational identity no longer serves.

Another general observation is that Protestants, while not denying that the Church is the Body of Christ, tend to emphasize God's saving work in individuals, whereas Catholics take a more communal view of salvation, seeing the Church as the instrument in and through which Christ, the "one Mediator between God and men," [209] ordinarily exercises His divine power in the world. Consequently, in the Catholic understanding, grace is mediated to the individual believer through the sacraments (five of which depend on the ordained priesthood),[210] the intercession of the saints, and even the reading and hearing of Scripture. Protestants, on the other hand, especially those who identify themselves as "evangelicals," regard all these secondary mediators (except for the Bible) as "getting in the way" between God and the Christian.

According to United Nations statistics, almost 400 million of the world's two billion Christians are Protestant; these include

---

[209] 1 Timothy 2:5.

[210] Namely: Confirmation, the Eucharist, Penance (or Reconciliation), the Anointing of the Sick, and Holy Orders. In case of emergency, anyone--even an unbaptized person--may baptize validly. As to the Sacrament of Marriage, Roman Catholic theology holds that the spouses are the ministers of the sacrament.

some 123 million in North America. Estimates place the number of Protestant denominations in the United States alone at more than 250, with approximately 35 percent of Americans identifying themselves as Protestant. The Lutheran, Reformed (Calvinist), and Anglican traditions have dominated world Protestantism, but in the United States it was the Radical wing (also variously known as Anabaptist, Nonconformist, or Free Church) that gained ascendancy, developing into the various Baptist, Congregationalist, Disciples of Christ, Mennonite, Adventist, and Pentecostal bodies. The issue of slavery in the mid-nineteenth century further split several American Protestant denominations into northern and southern branches.

The twenty largest Protestant denominations in the United States are: [211]

1. Southern Baptist Convention (16.2 million)
2. United Methodist Church (7.8 million)
3. Church of God in Christ (5.5 million)
4. National Baptist Convention USA, Inc. (5.0 million)
5. Evangelical Lutheran Church in America (4.5 million)
6. National Baptist Convention of America, Inc. (3.5 million)
7. Assemblies of God (2.9 million)
8. Presbyterian Church (USA) (2.8 million)
9. African Methodist Episcopal Church (2.5 million)
10. National Missionary Baptist Convention of America (2.5 million)
11. Lutheran Church—Missouri Synod (2.3 million)
12. Episcopal Church (2.0 million)
13. Churches of Christ (1.6 million)
14. Pentecostal Assemblies of the World, Inc. (1.5 million)
15. African Methodist Episcopal Zion Church (1.4 million)

---

[211] This list has been compiled from membership figures reported in the *Yearbook of American and Canadian Churches* 2011, ed. Eileen W. Linder (Nashville, Tenn.: Abingdon Press, 2011), published by the National Council of Churches USA. I have excluded the Church of Jesus Christ of Latter-day Saints (6.1 million), Jehovah's Witnesses (1.2 million), and the Seventh-Day Adventist Church (1.0 million) because these groups are really no more Protestant than Catholic; hence their classification in the present book as Christian offshoots. Also, I have rounded the figures to the nearest hundred thousand.

16. American Baptist Churches in the USA (1.3 million)
17. United Church of Christ (1.0 million)
18. Church of God (Cleveland, Tennessee) (1.1 million)
19. Christian Churches and Churches of Christ (1.1 million)
20. Progressive National Baptist Convention, Inc. (1.0 million)

Our survey of contemporary Protestantism will follow a taxonomic classification scheme, based on theological similarity and historical descent. Such a scheme enables us to see what groups are subsets of other groups. For instance, all Presbyterian denominations are grouped together because they belong to the Presbyterian denominational family, which is part of the Reformed branch of Protestantism. We will first cover the major branches stemming from the Reformation—the Lutheran, the Reformed, the Anglican, and the Radical (in that order)—and their respective denominational offshoots. Then we will turn to other forms of Protestantism having more recent, and peculiarly American, origin: Evangelicalism, with its "born again" enthusiasms, and Pentecostalism, with its emphasis on the continued manifestation of the gifts of the Holy Spirit.

The prevailing tendency of at least American Protestants has been to treat all churchly organization as a product of human creativity and an object of human manipulation. By contrast, Lutheranism provides a sense of catholicity by emphasizing the historic creeds, liturgical worship, and carefully constructed theology.

In the Reformed branch of Protestantism are many denominations, all strongly influenced by Calvinism. These are chiefly the Presbyterians and the various national Reformed Churches (Dutch Reformed, Swiss Reformed, Hungarian Reformed, etc.). The Baptists and Congregationalists can be seen as tributaries of the Reformed Churches, though both of these denominational families have roots also in the Radical wing. The United Church of Christ, an American denomination, was formed when several Congregationalist bodies merged with the "Evangelical and Reformed Church," itself an amalgamation of Lutherans and Calvinists. To some extent the anti-dogmatic Unitarians in the United States stemmed from the Congregationalists, although we must place Unitarianism in a different category.

Protestantism's third branch grew from the Anglican Church, or Church of England. Besides the Church of England, Anglicanism includes other self-governing Churches throughout the world. Its American branch is known as the Episcopal Church. Originating in the Church of England, yet no longer in communion with it, are the Methodists.

The Anabaptist movement formed the most radical wing of the Reformation. Among its denominational successors today are the Quakers and the old congregations set here and there on the checkerboard of America's farmland: the Amish, Mennonites, and Hutterites. The Puritans of England and their Baptist branch arose independently of Anabaptism but were clearly influenced by it, and some historians consider early Unitarianism as stemming from the Radical Reformation.

A final preliminary is needed before launching into contemporary Protestantism. According to Catholic doctrine, only those Christian communities which have preserved the apostolic succession of bishops and therefore possess a valid Eucharist are properly called "Churches"; all other Christian bodies are "ecclesial communities."[212] This may seem like a nit-picky point of semantics, but it is of a piece with the teaching of the Second Vatican Council that the Eucharist is "the source and summit" of the Church's life. More than the Church makes the Eucharist, the Eucharist makes the Church—and without the apostolic succession in ordained ministry, there is no valid Eucharist.

The separated Eastern Churches—Assyrian, Oriental Orthodox, and Eastern Orthodox—all merit the title "Church" because they have the ministerial priesthood and the Eucharist, even though they lack the ministry of Peter exercised by the Bishop of Rome. On the other hand, the Protestant communities are not "Church" in the proper sense, because they have not preserved the apostolic succession in ministry and are therefore deprived of a valid Eucharist, at least according to purely institutional criteria. (Unlike other Protestants, Anglicans insist they are "Church" in the Catholic sense, but the Catholic Church does

---

[212] Second Vatican Council, Decree on Ecumenism, *Unitatis Redintegratio*, nos. 3, 22. Reaffirmed by the Congregation for the Doctrine of the Faith in its Declaration *Dominus Iesus* (August 6, 2000), no. 17, and its *Responses to Some Questions Concerning Certain Aspects of the Doctrine of the Church* (June 29, 2007), q. 5.

not accept that claim.) Any reference in the present study to Protestant denominations as "churches" is intended merely in an analogous sense and as a convenient shorthand.

With these preliminary observations and necessary clarifications, we may begin to study the individual Protestant denominations whose churches gently jostle one another along the streets of the typical American town.

THE LUTHERANS

Numbering more than 70 million adherents, Lutheranism is the largest denominational family within worldwide Protestantism.[213] Most Lutheran denominations belong to the Lutheran World Federation (LWF), founded in 1947 in Sweden and headquartered in Geneva, Switzerland. Well more than half the world's Lutherans live in Germany and the countries of Scandinavia, where Lutheranism originally took root.

A distinguishing feature of Lutheranism is its affirmation of both "evangelical" and "catholic" ideas: a passion for the written and preached Word of God and the proclamation of forgiveness through faith in Christ's saving work, synthesized with a spiritual life centered on baptismal regeneration and belief in the Real Presence in the Eucharist. Traditional Lutheran worship is liturgical to a greater degree than that of most Protestants. The Lutheran Divine Service resembles the Catholic Mass from which it was adapted, minus the sacrificial vocabulary.

On the altar of a typical Lutheran church is either a crucifix or a plain cross, candles, the Bible, and flowers. Ministers wear the historic chasuble for the Divine Service and the cassock with surplice and stole for other liturgical ceremonies. An ecclesiastical calendar determines the liturgical color of the altar frontal and vestments: blue or purple for Advent, white or gold for Christmas and Easter, purple for Lent, scarlet for Passiontide, red for Pentecost, green for the Sundays after Epiphany and Pentecost, etc. Music—for the most part very good music—has always played a prominent part in Lutheran worship. Luther himself was a musician of note ("A Mighty Fortress Is Our God" being perhaps his most famous hymn), and not a few of Lutheranism's

---

[213] In keeping with the taxonomy explained in the previous section, the largest *branch* of global Protestantism is the Reformed, with more than 75 million.

thousands of hymns were composed by Johann Sebastian Bach, a devout Lutheran whose biblically inspired cantatas have been dubbed "the fifth Gospel."[214]

Lutherans make up the third largest Protestant denominational family in the United States, after the Baptists and Methodists. They are scarce in New England and the South, and strongest in the Midwest and Pennsylvania. The Evangelical Lutheran Church in America (ELCA), with 4.8 million members, and the Lutheran Church–Missouri Synod (LCMS), with 2.4 million, claim 80 percent of America's nine million Lutherans. The ELCA was created in 1988 after a series of mergers; German immigrants organized the much older LCMS in 1847.

Well into the twentieth century, American Lutherans were uncomfortable with their relation to other Protestants. Their relaxed attitude toward drinking, smoking, and dancing distinguished them from Baptists and other sects of Puritan extraction. At a time when most American Protestants were becoming strong advocates of public education, Lutherans established their own system of private schools. They were latecomers to the Protestant ecumenical movement, the foundations of which were laid at the World Missionary Conference held in Edinburgh, Scotland, in 1910. And, most significantly, they managed to avoid both the doctrinal laxity of the liberal Protestant mainline and the fundamentalism from which the evangelical movement emerged.

The divisions in present-day Lutheranism correspond to the general theological and political divisions in American Protestantism. From this perspective, the ELCA fits comfortably with the liberal mainline, while the LCMS looks like a branch of conservative evangelicalism. The ELCA ordains women and is squishy on abortion, premarital sex, and cohabitation. In 2009, its leadership decided to permit homosexual persons in "life-long, monogamous relationships" to serve as clergy and lay leaders, prompting some congregations to break with the ELCA and form a new denomination, the North American Lutheran Church (NALC). ELCA Lutherans are in full communion with six other liberal denominations: the Episcopal Church, the United Methodist Church, the United Church of Christ, the Reformed Church

---

[214] The term is credited to Swedish archbishop Nathan Söderblom (1866–1931).

in America, the Presbyterian Church USA, and the Moravian Church. These bodies agree to "pulpit sharing," intercommunion, and common decision-making on important matters.

Far less accommodating of modern secular culture is the defiantly orthodox and increasingly sectarian LCMS. Its original members were immigrants from Luther's own province of Saxony who landed near Saint Louis, Missouri, in 1839. These "Old Lutherans" opposed the merger of the Lutheran and Reformed churches in their homeland. Here they built their own parochial school system from kindergarten to university, and today they operate hundreds of schools, including Valparaiso University in Indiana and Concordia Seminary in Saint Louis. Insistence by some Missouri Synod leaders on biblical literalism caused a rupture in the mid–1970s, which eventually led to the formation of the ELCA. Some LCMS congregations have adopted the emotional and improvised style of worship commonly found in charismatic and nondenominational "Bible churches."

As the ELCA fades into the potpourri of liberal Protestantism and the LCMS edges toward evangelicalism, it remains to be seen whether Lutherans at both ends of the spectrum can or even want to maintain a distinct Lutheran identity. In the struggle to hold the orthodox center, some Lutherans, especially those who style themselves "evangelical catholics," have reached the conclusion that what makes Lutheranism Lutheran is ultimately unsustainable apart from Catholicism. In a divided Christianity, observed C. S. Lewis keenly, "those at the heart of each division are all closer to one another than those at the fringes."[215]

The Lutheran Reformation, unlike other Protestants who thought they were restoring the true Church, never intended to be anything but a reforming movement within the one Catholic Church. A momentous achievement in the quest for Christian unity was the "Joint Declaration on Justification by Faith," signed in 1999 by representatives of the LWF and the Catholic Church. It emphasizes that God accepts us by grace alone through faith in Christ and not on the basis of our merit; yet God's saving action in Christ calls us to live a life of faith, hope,

[215] William Griffin, *Clive Staples Lewis: A Dramatic Life* (San Francisco: Harper & Row, 1986), p. 336.

and charity. There are kinks to be worked out, certainly, and other Lutheran differences with Catholicism remain. Nonetheless, substantial consensus has been reached on the issue that sparked the Reformation. The ever-present question is whether there are compelling reasons in those remaining differences for maintaining the separation.

THE PRESBYTERIAN AND REFORMED CHURCHES

From present-day Lutheranism we turn to the Reformed branch of Protestantism. Since there is no consensus on the meaning of the term "Reformed," it is not easy to know how many groups belong to this category. Reformed Christianity has usually been taken to mean the churches originating in the work of Calvin, but this definition has lost some of its usefulness. For one thing, classical Calvinist theology, with its doctrines of double predestination and limited atonement, nowadays carries little weight in most churches claiming Calvin as their father. Further, recent scholarship views the Reformed tradition as the product of multiple influences and not simply the outworking of Calvin's own theology.[216] Further still, some denominations stemming from Calvinism have, as a result of mergers, been grafted onto branches of Protestantism other than the Reformed.

For our purposes, we shall define Reformed Christianity broadly, to encompass all denominations having historic roots in the Calvinist-influenced Reformation except for Anglicanism, which constitutes a category of its own. When Calvinists organized churches on the European continent they called them Reformed. In the British Isles and North America these churches were named Presbyterian to describe their form of government. But alongside this came a brand of Protestantism, for the most part Calvinist, which insisted on the absolute autonomy of each local congregation and democracy in governance: Congregationalism. From this group emerged the Baptists, whose views on Baptism and the Church were less akin to Calvin's than to those of the radical Anabaptists.

[216] For example: Richard Muller, *After Calvin: Studies in the Development of a Theological Tradition* (New York: Oxford University Press, 2003); idem, "John Calvin and Later Calvinism: The Identity of the Reformed Tradition," in *The Cambridge Companion to Reformation Theology*, ed. David Bagchi and David C. Steinmetz (Cambridge, Eng.: Cambridge University Press, 2004), pp. 130–149.

The Reformed/Presbyterian family predominates in Scotland, Northern Ireland, and the Netherlands and claims large memberships also in Switzerland, South Africa, Germany, and Hungary. As a result of Arian and Unitarian heresies, Presbyterianism in England crumbled in the eighteenth century; only later Scottish immigration saved Presbyterianism from extinction there. With the rapid expansion of missionary activity after 1800, Reformed and Presbyterian churches were established in Asia, Africa, Latin America, and the East Indies. The Geneva-based World Alliance of Reformed Churches (WARC), established in 1970, was a fellowship of 75 million Christians in more than one hundred countries, representing more than two hundred Reformed, Presbyterian, Congregationalist, and United denominations. In June 2010, it merged with the much smaller Reformed Ecumenical Council (REC) to create the World Communion of Reformed Churches (WCRC).

Reformed orthodox theology has been framed by a great number of confessional statements, written by different people in different places: the Gallic Confession (1559), the Scots Confession (1560), the Belgic Confession (1561), the Heidelberg Catechism (1563), the Westminster Confession (1646), and so on. Although there is consistency in the fundamental content of these confessions, Reformed Christians recognize no one confession as an absolute, infallible statement of their faith. The Westminster Confession remains the standard of faith for Anglo-American Presbyterianism, but its statement on predestination has been drastically modified to bring it much closer to the Catholic position. One would have to look to the tiny Presbyterian sects to hear predestination preached as it was in Calvin's Geneva.

Puritan ministers brought Presbyterianism to America when they followed the dissenters out of the Church of England. Some switched to Congregationalism in the Massachusetts Bay Colony, while others remained Presbyterians. Reformed theology played a specific role in founding of the United States, according to Constitutional attorney Doug Phillips: "It was there [Geneva] that [Calvin's] careful articulation of Christian theology as applied to familial, civil, and ecclesiastical authority modeled many of the principles of liberty later embraced by our own Founders, including anti-statism, the belief in transcendent principles of law as the foundation of an ethical legal system, free market economics, decentralized authority, an educated citizenry as a safeguard against tyranny, and republican representative government which was accountable to the people and a higher law."[217] Nearly all Presbyterians backed the American Revolution, which in England was called "the Presbyterian Rebellion." Twelve of the 55 signers of the Declaration of Independence were Presbyterians, including the only clergyman to sign: John Witherspoon.

In the United States today, Presbyterianism is largely English, Scottish, and Scotch-Irish. It has traditionally been strong in New York, New Jersey, and Pennsylvania, but enrolls large memberships in the Midwest and California. Some sixty American colleges and universities, including Princeton, are affiliated with the Presbyterian Church.

Each Presbyterian congregation elects ruling presbyters or elders and a teaching elder; the latter is the minister but is theoretically on a par with the other elders. The pastor and ruling elders are supervised by the regional body, or presbytery, to which it belongs. The presbytery, composed of all the ministers and one ruling elder from each church, ordains candidates for the ministry, installs and removes pastors, settles disciplinary and doctrinal questions, and starts new churches. Synods, usually organized along state lines, do for the presbyteries what the presbyteries do for the local churches: the member presbyteries elect an equal number of ministers and ruling elders to the synod, which meets annually. Topping the Presbyterian structure in each country is the General Assembly, which includes an equal number of pastors and elders from each presbytery; its powers include the right to reorganize synods, settle disputes, and ratify mergers with other denominations.

Ninety percent of American Presbyterians belong to three denominations: the Presbyterian Church USA (PCUSA), with 2.3 million members; the Presbyterian Church in America, numbering 279,000; and the 87,000-member Cumberland Presbyterian Church. The PCUSA was created in 1983 from the merger of the United Presbyterian Church and the Presbyterian Church in the United States. In the early 1970s, some 41,000 people left the

---

[217] Doug Phillips, "John Calvin, Founding Father," *The Washington Post* online (*onfaith.washingtonpost.com*), posted July 7, 2009.

latter denomination in protest of its leaders' support for abortion rights and other liberal causes; they formed the Presbyterian Church in America, which today provides a conservative alternative to the PCUSA. The PCUSA's decision, in July 2011, to ordain actively homosexual clergy prompted more than two thousand opponents to form a new denomination, the Evangelical Covenant Order of Presybyterians, in January 2012.

THE CONGREGATIONALISTS AND THE "UNITED CHURCH OF CHRIST"

The Congregationalists are the spiritual descendants of the Puritans who left England to create a godly commonwealth in the New World. Strict Calvinists all, the Puritans criticized the established Church of England as insufficiently Protestantized. Most Puritans sought to "purify" the national Church from within, but a separatist minority had given up on official Anglicanism. The Puritans were divided also over ecclesiastical polity: the nonseparatists were mostly Presbyterians while the separatists insisted on a Church "without pope, prelate, presbytery, prince, or parliament."

When the first substantial body of Puritans arrived at the Massachusetts Bay Colony in the early 1630s, the smaller Plymouth colony to the south had already been in place for a decade. The Plymouth settlement was a separatist Puritan outpost. These Puritans had fled persecution in England for the greater tolerance found in the Netherlands, but after watching their children take on Dutch ways, they looked farther afield for a place where they might be left alone. About forty of the separatists (with sixty others to fill up the ship) embarked on the Mayflower for an ill-defined North American destination. These "Pilgrims" arrived at Cape Cod Bay in November 1620, and before the first winter was past, half their tiny band had died from cold, starvation, or disease.

The Presbyterian Puritans of the Massachusetts Bay Colony eventually adopted the Congregationalism of their Plymouth neighbors. In 1691, the two settlements merged and Congregationalism became the established religion in New England. Each congregation could adopt the Apostles' Creed, compose a creed of its own, or remain creedless. Given its theological basis in Calvinism, Congregationalist worship was severely plain: lengthy sermons, Bible reading, unadorned churches, and the singing of psalms only. It was forbidden to observe the "popish" holiday of Christmas. Today Christmas finds a place in the Congregationalist year, as does the Puritans' own contribution to the calendar, Thanksgiving Day. Hymns and organs gradually were introduced, and the service was shortened.

Like their Presbyterian counterparts, Congregationalists always have valued higher learning. Church members founded Harvard, Yale, Dartmouth, Bowdoin, Amherst, Smith, and many other colleges, most of which have since passed from church control. After the Civil War, they set up hundreds of schools for blacks in the former Confederate states.

Early on, the Congregationalist establishment had given birth to a radical, anti-doctrinal movement, and by the end of the eighteenth century Congregationalists, both in England and America, were divided into two parties: Trinitarian and Unitarian. The Unitarians gained control of Harvard, the original Pilgrim church at Plymouth, and all but one of Boston's fourteen congregations.

Another reason for Congregationalism's decline was the Plan of Union of 1801, an agreement between Congregationalists and Presbyterians to cooperate in missionary endeavors but usually worked to the latter's advantage. Two thousand Congregationalist churches outside New England were lost to the better-organized Presbyterians.

In 1931, the Congregationalists merged with the 100,000-member "Christian Church," sometimes known as the Baptist Unitarians, who denied the divinity of Christ and rejected all creeds. The new denomination initially called itself the "Congregational and Christian Churches" but later dropped the "and."

Congregationalism remained primarily a New England institution until 1957, when the General Council of Congregational Christian Churches merged with the Evangelical and Reformed Church (ERC) to form the United Church of Christ (UCC), whose current membership hovers at around one million. At the time of that merger, the Congregational Christian Churches counted 1.3 million adult members, 60 percent of the total number of members in the new denomination.

By the 1950s, denominational mergers were nothing new in American Protestantism. The ERC was itself a fusion, having been organized by the 1934 union of two German-American denominations: the Evangelical Synod of North America, composed of congregations of mixed Lutheran and Reformed heritage, and the older Reformed Church in the United States (RCUS), founded by immigrants from the Palatinate and other German districts where Calvinism prevailed. Three distinguished twentieth-century American Protestant theologians were ERC ministers: Paul Tillich and the brothers Reinhold and H. Richard Niebuhr.

The UCC was a unique breed. Congregationalism came to these shores with the Pilgrims and became a virtual theocracy in New England; the ERC found its adherents among the descendants of German immigrants in Pennsylvania and the Midwest. Congregationalists refused to bind members with creeds; the ERC upheld both the Lutheran Augsburg Confession and the Reformed Heidelberg Catechism. Congregationalism demanded complete autonomy for each congregation; the ERC was presbyterian in polity.

Not everyone went along with the various mergers. Four hundred Congregational churches chose not to merge with the ERC and retain the Congregational name. The RCUS still exists and is one of many "continuing" Reformed groups. In New England and in other parts of the country, the local UCC church may still label itself Congregational.

Arguably the most liberal church on the American scene, the UCC supports the abortion license, operates a condom distribution "ministry," and endorses same-sex "marriage." It ran television ads about its inclusiveness, contrasting itself with churches where "others" are supposedly unwelcome. One commercial depicted a single black mother with her crying baby, a homosexual couple, and an Arab-looking man being propelled out of a church by ejection seats attached to the pews; it concluded with the line, "The United Church of Christ. No matter who you are or where you are on life's journey, you're welcome here."

Nothing wrong with that, so long as inclusiveness in Christ's name include also those who prefer an identifiably Christian view of things. Then again, such people are more likely to belong to churches where the Gospel call to conversion trumps lifestyle liberalisms.

Historians have isolated two distinct beginnings of the Baptist movement: the General Baptists, who evolved out of a church started by John Smyth, a Puritan Separatist who re-baptized himself and his exiled congregation at Amsterdam in 1609; and the Particular Baptists, who arose among the underground London congregations of the 1630s. The General Baptists, holding with the Dutch theologian Jacob Arminius (1560–1609), believed that Christ died indiscriminately for all persons; the Particular Baptists, on the other hand, were rigid Calvinists who held that Christ died for the elect only. In the early decades of their coexistence, the debates between Arminian and Calvinist Baptists were intense. The same debates were replayed among Baptists in America.

Early English Baptist authors include John Bunyan (*Pilgrim's Progress*), John Milton (*Paradise Lost*), and Daniel Defoe (*Robinson Crusoe*).

The Baptist Confession of 1678 incorporated the Apostles', Nicene-Constantinopolitan, and Athanasian creeds, declaring that all three "may be proved by most undoubted authority of Holy Scripture and are necessary to be understood of all Christians." Reflecting this same impulse, the Baptists who gathered in London for the inaugural meeting of the Baptist World Alliance in 1905 stood in that assembly and recited in unison the Apostles' Creed.

A memorable acronym for the key Baptist principles, most of which are shared with other Protestants, is BAPTIST: Biblical authority, Autonomy of the local church (congregationalism), Priesthood of all believers, Two "ordinances" (Baptism and the Lord's Supper, understood as symbols, not sacraments), Individual "soul competency" (the God-given ability of each person to know and respond to God's will, without coercion by any religious or civil body), Separation of church and state (a corollary of soul competency), and Two church orders only (pastors and deacons).

Although Baptists are historically linked to English Puritanism, which was more or less Calvinist, their distinctive doctrine regarding Baptism derives from the Anabaptists of the Radical Reformation. Baptists believe that Baptism is not a means of grace—a sacrament—but rather a testimony of the believer's voluntary faith by which he has already received salvation; hence, infants and others incapable of personal faith are ineligible for Baptism, called "Believer's Baptism." Likewise, Baptists recognize immersion (the dipping of the person in water), rather than pouring or sprinkling, as the only proper mode of Baptism, because immersion vividly expresses the meaning of Baptism as a burial with Christ in the waters of death and a rising with Christ to new life.[218]

Roger Williams (1603–1683) founded the first Baptist church in America. Educated at Cambridge and ordained in the established Church of England, Williams became, in turn, a Puritan (Congregationalist, still within the Anglican Church), Separatist, Baptist, and "Seeker." He left England in 1630 and sought religious freedom in the Massachusetts Bay Colony, where he was banished for his beliefs in religious liberty and strict Church-State separation. On the basis of a Narragansett Indian deed, he took title to a tract some seventy miles west of Cape Cod, in what is today Rhode Island, settling himself at a place the natives called Seekonk, which he renamed Providence. By 1639, the church he organized there was practicing Believer's Baptism, Williams having been re-baptized by a church member. A few months later, he resigned his pastorate and resumed his quest for religious truth until his death. The historic church still stands on College Hill in Providence.

Sixteen million Americans belong to churches affiliated with the Southern Baptist Convention (SBC), the largest Protestant denomination in the United States. Originally confined to the states of the old Confederacy, Southern Baptist churches can now be found throughout the nation, outnumbering all other churches in most southern and southwestern states. The SBC supports thousands of missionaries in home and foreign missions.

The American Baptist Churches in the USA (called Northern Baptist until 1950), with 1.3 million faithful, have mirrored the

---

[218] See Romans 6:3–5; Colossians 2:12.

membership decline of the other mainline churches. To this liberal denomination belongs the First Baptist Church in the city of Providence.

Seventh-Day Baptists, counting some 50,000 members in more than twenty countries, observe Saturday rather than Sunday as the Sabbath day. Their first congregation was established in Newport, Rhode Island, in 1671.

Free Will Baptists, organized in North Carolina in 1727 and in New Hampshire in 1780, are the American heirs of the English General Baptists. The issue of slavery, and later the Civil War, divided the group. In 1910, the northern Free Will Baptists merged with the Northern Baptist Convention, while those in the South maintained their separate existence until 1935.

In the 1980s and 1990s, the SBC underwent a major upheaval and reorientation resulting from a strong movement to retrieve the Calvinist tradition in Baptist life. The moderates, called "liberals" by their opponents, attribute this development to the attractiveness of dogmatic certainty in an age of rapid change. The conservatives, called "fundamentalists" by their opponents, cite renewed interest in what the Bible teaches about salvation, grace, and election. In point of fact, a strongly Calvinist undercurrent has always run just beneath the surface of traditional Baptist piety, as is evident in every Baptist's favorite hymn, "Amazing Grace." Since the conservative resurgence, the SBC has become increasingly sectarian and isolationist.

By defying the apostolic Tradition of baptizing infants and of never rebaptizing, Baptists have carried Protestant principles to conclusions the sixteenth-century Reformers, including Calvin, hesitated to draw. When one considers that the original Reformers preserved a sacramental view of Baptism and appealed to the Church Fathers in defense of their views, there is reason to hope that efforts to recover the Reformation roots of the Baptist heritage might also move in the opposite direction, toward a more fully orbed Christian orthodoxy.

THE "DISCIPLES OF CHRIST" AND ITS OFFSHOOTS

The early years of the nineteenth century saw the rise of the largest Christian movement born on American soil: the Restoration Movement, also called the Stone-Campbell Movement, named after Barton W. Stone (1772–1844) and Alexander Campbell (1788–1866). Its goal was to overcome denominationalism and "restore" the true Church of the New Testament. Paradoxically, that effort contributed more denominations to the roster of Protestant sects.

Alexander Campbell, son of Thomas Campbell, a Presbyterian minister, was born in Ireland. Educated in Ireland and at Glasgow University, he immigrated to America in 1809 with his mother and siblings, where they reunited with the elder Campbell, who had settled in western Pennsylvania. He joined in his father's rejection of Presbyterianism and organized an independent church at Brush Run. Persuaded that adult Baptism by immersion was the only valid Baptism, the Campbells were rebaptized in 1812 and entered into fellowship with the Baptists. Alexander founded (1823) and edited (until 1830) the *Christian Baptist*, a widely circulated monthly.

For all their rhetoric about "Scripture alone," the original Protestants of the sixteenth century, like the Baptists after them, not only affirmed the dogmas of the early Church in the language of the ancient creeds, but also added to these classic statements their own particular confessions of faith. But Campbell would have "no creed but Christ." All religious authority was reduced to a simple maxim: "Where the Bible speaks, we speak; where the Bible is silent, we are silent." Believing it was possible and desirable to strip Christianity of all post-New Testament accretions, he permitted only *a cappella* singing in church, because the New Testament makes no mention of instrumental music in Christian worship.

By the late 1820s, the Baptists had had enough of Campbell's primitivism, and the Campbellites (the nickname dates to 1832) were being forced out of Baptist churches. At Campbell's suggestion, his followers formed congregations and called themselves Disciples of Christ. They were attracted by a similarity of purpose to the "Christians" in Kentucky led by Barton Warren Stone, a Maryland-born ex-Presbyterian, and in 1832 the two movements united to form the "Christian Church (Disciples of Christ)."

Since Campbell neither supported nor condemned slavery, the

Disciples managed to avoid schism during the Civil War, giving them an advantage over the sundered Baptists, Presbyterians, and Methodists. However, they were not spared the controversies over biblical authority and interpretation that split many Protestant churches around the turn of the twentieth century. In 1906, the fundamentalist wing separated from the Disciples to form the "Churches of Christ."

The breakaway of the Churches of Christ was not the only schism in the Restoration Movement. A desire for a stronger national organization led to a restructuring of the Disciples of Christ in 1968. Opponents of the move saw it as the "last straw" of a decades-long slide into denominationalism; they left the Disciples and organized the "Christian Churches and Churches of Christ," also known as the "Independent Christian Churches."[219]

Most of the 700,000 Disciples live in half a dozen southern and Midwestern states. Like the other two Restorationist branches, Disciples baptize by immersion and pride themselves on remaining creedless. No Disciple, minister or layperson, need affirm belief in any specific Christian doctrine. Unlike many Protestants, Disciples observe the Lord's Supper every Sunday. Local Disciples churches may choose to join district and state conferences. Most churches belong to the Disciples of Christ International Convention, with headquarters in Indianapolis. Disciples colleges include Bethany in West Virginia, founded by Alexander Campbell in 1840, and Texas Christian in Fort Worth.

With an estimated membership of one million, the Churches of Christ is more loosely organized than the Disciples. The closest thing to a convention is the annual Bible lectureship on the campus of Abilene Christian College, which draws as many as ten thousand people. Among the other Churches of Christ institutions are Pepperdine (California), Harding (Arkansas), Faulkner (Alabama), and Lipscomb (Tennessee). Churches of Christ congregations exist throughout the United States and in many other countries, but membership is concentrated in Tennessee, West Virginia, the Ozark regions of Missouri and Arkansas, and the plains of central Texas. Rejection of instrumental music in worship is a test of fellowship.

---

[219] The official denominational names are here placed in quotation marks for the sake of clarity.

The "undenominational" Christian Churches and Churches of Christ, with just above one million members, stands to the "right" of the theologically liberal Disciples and to the "left" of the fundamentalist Churches of Christ. It sponsors an extensive missionary program in more than fifty countries, and operates eighteen liberal arts and Bible colleges, the two largest being Lincoln (Illinois) Christian and Cincinnati Christian. The heartland of its strength is approximately the same as that of the Disciples of Christ: from western Pennsylvania across the Midwest to Missouri and Iowa, but with sizable membership also in Kentucky, northern California, and the Pacific Northwest.

Attempting to distinguish among the churches of the three Restorationist branches is enough to make one's head spin. Disciples churches seldom include the word "Disciples" in their name and are usually known simply as "Christian" (for example, "First Christian Church" or "Davis Street Christian Church"). Likewise, many independent congregations go by the name "Christian Church." Some Disciples churches use the term "Church of Christ," but so do most Churches of Christ churches and many congregations of the Independent Christian Churches fellowship. In the quest for the true Church of Christ, names are unpersuasive.

Rather than delivering Christians from disunity, Campbell's efforts to restore apostolic Christianity increased their divisions. There is but one basis for union: the inherited truths of the Gospel as they are doctrinally interpreted within the one Church of the Bible and of the creeds.

THE ANGLICANS (EPISCOPALIANS)

From the Reformed tradition and its derivatives—the Baptists, Disciples, and Churches of Christ—we turn now to Anglicanism, which in many respects seeks to mediate between Catholicism and Protestantism. Earlier we noted that the Church of England resulted not from theological disputes but from a king's desire to have his marriage annulled. As the establishment of the Church of England arose from political concerns, so too did the shaping of its theological identity. The strong claims of both Catholic and Protestant beliefs in Reformation England led to the Elizabethan Settlement, a politically astute, if theologically nebulous, compromise between the two theological perspectives.

This theological identity accounts for the great diversity of beliefs and forms within Anglicanism. Church historian Diarmaid MacCulloch (Oxford) characterizes Anglicanism as a "mood" that makes a virtue of uncertainty.[220] But even in the midst of this confusion, Anglicanism's history, from Cranmer's 1549 *Book of Common Prayer* through the sixteenth-and seventeenth-century Anglican divines (leading writers and clergy), reveals an emphasis on the authority of early Church councils and the Church Fathers, more so than most continental Protestant theologians. And unlike the other Protestant bodies, Anglicans value and claim the apostolic succession of bishops.

The worldwide Anglican Communion of 70 million Christians comprises a number of independent sister Churches largely confined to Britain and to former British colonies. Its two largest provinces are the Church of Nigeria (15 million) and the Church of Uganda (9 million). No figures are available for England specifically (rather than the United Kingdom as a whole); the Church of England puts the number of regular churchgoers at just under two million.

The Archbishop of Canterbury is primate of the Church of England and spiritual head of Anglicanism. The king or queen is technically the Supreme Governor of the Church of England, but the prime minister, who need not be an Anglican or even a Christian, appoints the Archbishop of Canterbury. Every ten years, the Archbishop of Canterbury invites all Anglican bishops to meet at his residence, Lambeth Palace.

British colonists brought Anglicanism to these shores in the Virginia settlement of 1607. Wholly dependent on the mother Church of England, the American branch had no bishop or diocesan organization for 177 years. Candidates for the priesthood risked smallpox and shipwreck to return to England for ordination, and the colonials were unable to receive confirmation until after the American Revolution. At the outbreak of the Revolution, most Anglican clergymen fled to England and Canada

---

[220] Diarmaid MacCulloch, "The Birth of Anglicanism," *Ecclesiastical Law Journal* 7 (2004): 418–428.

because they had taken an oath of loyalty to the king. Before the hostilities, the mother Church had been supported by taxes in the southern colonies. With this financial support gone, its clergy scattered, and its name associated with tyranny, the Anglican Church in America faced serious postwar problems. It lost many members to the energetic Baptists, Congregationalists, and Methodists. A General Convention in Philadelphia in 1789 united the Anglicans in the newly formed United States into the Protestant Episcopal Church (the word "Protestant" was dropped in 1967). As in colonial times, the Episcopal Church finds its chief strength on the Eastern seaboard.

Both the Episcopal Church and the wider Anglican Communion have faced many crises in recent decades. In the mid–1970s, the Episcopal Church unilaterally decided to ordain women to the priesthood, and the Church of England followed suit. At about the same time, it adopted permissive attitudes toward abortion and divorce. The Episcopal Church then ordained women to the episcopate. Further commotion was sparked by the consecration of Gene Robinson, a partnered homosexual, as Episcopal bishop of New Hampshire in 2003. A number of Anglican provinces, notably in Africa and Asia (where the great majority of Anglicans are), have declared that they are no longer in communion with the American church. The Church of England decided to allow women bishops in 2010.

While on the subject of ordination, the Catholic Church maintains that Scripture and Tradition do not authorize the ordination of women as priests. If the ordination of women priests is invalid, the ordination of women bishops casts a broader pall of invalidity, because bishops ordain priests. Aside from the matter of sex, Pope Leo XIII declared in 1896 that Anglican holy orders are null and void,[221] a decision that still stands. The reason, in short order, is that under the reign of Edward VI (1547–1553) Archbishop Cranmer cut the sacrificial heart out of the Mass and revised the ordination rite to exclude mention of the priest's sacrificial function. By Catholic standards, a church that denies a sacrificing priesthood cannot pass on the priesthood. The defective ordination rite was used until 1662, by which time all validly

[221] Leo XIII, Apostolic Letter *Apostolicae Curae* (September 13, 1896).

ordained Anglican bishops had died, and the apostolic succession in ministry was broken.

Disaffected Episcopalians have formed at least a dozen breakaway churches over these and other controversial issues. From a high of 3.6 million communicants in 1966 the Episcopal Church now numbers two million, one of the largest declines of any denomination, except perhaps the Disciples of Christ.

In 2009, Pope Benedict XVI provided for "personal ordinariates" that would allow Anglicans to enter the Catholic Church while maintaining elements of their distinctive spiritual and liturgical tradition, including the ordination of married former Anglican clergy as Catholic priests.[222] The Anglican liturgy has behind it a long tradition, stretching back further than the past several centuries of Anglicanism itself. Because it reflects in some ways an essentially monastic approach to theology,[223] it can broaden what has been, at least in the past century or so, a rather narrowly defined Catholic liturgical landscape.

THE METHODISTS

The Methodists trace their roots to the dynamic ministry of John Wesley (1703–1791), a devout Anglican priest aided by his brother Charles (1707–1788), also an Anglican priest and a talented hymn-writer ("Hark! the Herald Angels Sing" and "Christ the Lord Is Risen Today," to name just two gems). While young students at Oxford, the brothers organized a "Holy Club" whose rules included fasting on Fridays, Bible reading, weekly Communion, almsgiving, and visiting the sick and imprisoned. Because of the group's methodical approach to prayer and temperance, scoffers dubbed them "Methodists."

In his student days John Wesley did not like the excessive emphasis placed on justification by faith. As biographer Stephen Tomkins explains, "He had an evangelical horror of trying to satisfy God by good works, but an even greater horror of trying

---

[222] Benedict XVI, Apostolic Constitution *Anglicanorum Coetibus* (November 4, 2009).

[223] See John-Bede Pauley, "The Implication of Monastic Qualities on the Pastoral Provision for the Anglican Use," *Antiphon: A Journal for Liturgical Renewal* 10:3 (2006): 261–276.

[224] Stephen Tomkins, *John Wesley: A Biography* (Grand Rapids, Mich.: Wm. B. Eerdmans, 2003), p. 196.

to satisfy God without good works."[224] While admitting that salvation is pure gift, he also knew that faith is valueless without charity, and so he came to advocate his most distinctive doctrine, claiming—against Saint Augustine, Luther, and Calvin—that perfect holiness is attainable in this life. Wesley's insistence that holiness is the substance of religion (with faith but its portal) soon gave rise to the various "Holiness churches," and these later gave birth to Pentecostalism, now the world's fastest-growing Christian movement.

In 1735, Wesley was sent to Georgia to head a missionary society. Things went badly, and after two years he returned to England. Preaching in private homes, fields, barns, public squares, and wherever a crowd assembled to hear him, Wesley inspired people of all social classes to make a personal commitment to Christ. Once, when someone protested that outdoor services were unbecoming an Anglican clergyman, Wesley responded: "To save souls is my vocation; all the world is my parish." Britain alone would prove enough of a challenge. Wesley covered 250,000 miles on foot and horseback throughout the nation, preaching no fewer than forty thousand sermons.

Relations between Wesley and the Anglican hierarchs, many of whom dismissed the Methodists as sanctimonious zealots, were often strained, and by the end of his days a break with his beloved Church of England seemed inevitable. Indeed, Wesley himself provoked the split, which took place only after his death, when on his own authority he ordained missionaries for America. That move, which brother Charles denounced, meant a de facto break. Wesley justified his actions by claiming that bishops and priests were identical in the primitive Church.

Again acting on his own authority, Wesley dropped fifteen of Anglicanism's "Thirty-Nine Articles," most of which pertained to justification. Other sources of Methodist belief are Wesley's *Notes on the New Testament* and collected sermons. Wesley's rejection of predestination in the Calvinist sense, his insistence on good works, his encouragement of devotional practices and frequent Communion: all these distinguished Methodism from Calvinist traditions found in the Reformed Churches.

Although Methodism had a slow start in the American colonies, within ten years after the close of the Revolutionary War it had adapted itself to the new nation more successfully than any other religion. From a constituency of a few thousand at the time of the war, Methodists grew to constitute the largest religious group in the United States by 1800. Catholics and Baptists would later outnumber them, but the United Methodist Church, with more than seven million members, is the third largest communion in the United States.

The key to Methodism's success in America, as in Britain, was its missionary core. Circuit riders carried the Gospel to the edges of the frontier, while in the growing cities of the East, Methodist chapels were crowded with factory-workers, artisans, slum-dwellers, and slaves. Methodism welcomed blacks and women into its ranks, and even elevated some to leadership positions. It sought out people with little or no religious upbringing and offered them a warm, emotional message. And unlike the earlier Puritans, Methodists did not spend much time in brooding self-examination. Their emphasis on free will appealed to optimistic, upward-aspiring Americans at a time when self-improvement was itself becoming a religion. Today, Methodists in the United States run more hospitals and institutions of higher learning than any other Protestant group. Among the one hundred colleges and universities affiliated, or once affiliated, with Methodism are Boston University, Drew, Duke, Emory, Southern Methodist, and Syracuse.

Although Wesley prescribed weekly Communion, not all Methodist churches today observe the Lord's Supper every Sunday. The optional "Service of Word and Table," as outlined in the United Methodist Book of Worship, is set in a fourfold movement of Entrance, Proclamation and Response, Thanksgiving and Communion, and Sending Forth.

The World Methodist Council, founded in 1881 and headquartered at Lake Junaluska in North Carolina, represents 70 million members of Methodist and related United churches "in the Wesleyan tradition." Church authority rests with the General Conference. This body, consisting of equal numbers of locally elected laypersons and ministers, meets every four years; its decisions are incorporated into the "Book of Discipline." Church polity in the United States is episcopal, although the difference between bishops and other ministers is purely one of administrative responsibility. United Methodism's executive branch is the Council of Bishops; its chief legislative branch, the General Conference; and its highest court, the Judicial Council.

The lines of division within Methodism track the liberal/conservative divide within the Protestant mainline. In recent decades the United Methodist Church has repeatedly turned back the advocates of legitimizing homosexuality. Delegates at the 2008 General Conference affirmed sexual relations "only within the covenant of monogamous, heterosexual marriage." At stake, as ever, is the role of Scripture and Tradition in the formation of Christian conscience.

THE HOLINESS AND PENTECOSTAL CHURCHES

Methodism's founder, JOHN Wesley, believed that perfect holiness is attainable in this life. In his model of the order of salvation, a Christian can receive a subsequent blessing after justification that bestows perfect liberation from all sin, including sinful thoughts. This teaching is called Christian perfection or "entire sanctification." In the 1820s and 1830s, evangelist Charles Finney popularized the doctrine of entire sanctification. But whereas Wesley held that perfection is normally preceded by a lengthy period of spiritual maturation, Finney taught that it instantaneously follows conversion.

By the 1860s, entire sanctification was seldom mentioned in Methodist churches. When religious revivals rekindled interest in the doctrine, a national "Holiness movement" arose in Methodism; its proponents became known as "holy rollers." Criticism by Methodist bishops led to the formation of independent Holiness churches in the 1890s. Then and now, these churches are characterized by emotionalism, swingy Gospel hymns, faith healing, and a Puritanical moral code.

The largest body of the Holiness movement is the Church of the Nazarene, formed in 1908 from the merger of several smaller sects whose members were drawn from Methodism. Headquartered in Lenexa, Kansas, this denomination closely resembles Methodism in doctrine, worship, and polity. The Nazarenes report a worldwide membership of more than 1.5 million, mostly in the United States, Haiti, and India.

Other Holiness groups include the Free Methodist Church,

the Wesleyan Church, and the Christian and Missionary Alliance. None of these started off as denominations but rather as movements or parachurch organizations. Membership growth in the sundry Holiness churches continues to surpass the mainline Protestant denominations. Pentecostalism, however, is the world's fastest growing Christian movement.

With deep roots in the Holiness tradition and African spirituality, Pentecostalism began at the turn of the twentieth century. Charles Fox Parham (1873–1929), a Methodist minister in the Holiness movement and founder of Bethel Bible College in Topeka, Kansas, became convinced that the story of Pentecost in chapter 2 of the Acts of the Apostles is not only a description of what happened to the first generation of Christians. Rather, it is a blueprint of what should happen in every generation of the Church. All Christians, Parham asserted, can and should experience "Baptism in the Holy Spirit," which is distinct from and follows water Baptism. This second "baptism" bestows all the gifts of Pentecost and is evidenced by "speaking in tongues," or *glossolalia*: sounds and syllables uttered under the direction of the Holy Spirit. The meaning of these utterances is completely unintelligible to both the speaker and most hearers. Comprehension requires an additional intervention of God known as "the interpretation of tongues."[225]

Parenthetically, medieval commentators on the Bible understood the gift of interpretation of tongues quite differently, as an ability either to translate from one known language into another (Hebrew into Latin, for example) or to explain obscure Scripture passages.[226] This is not to say that they denied that miraculous, ecstatic utterances took place on the day of Pentecost, or that they discounted the possibility of such miracles in special circumstances.

The first incident of glossolalic utterance was at Bethel Bible in 1901. Soon many of the students as well as Parham were speaking in tongues. For the next few years, Parham and his students carried the "Pentecostal" message to various communities in the South and Southwest. In 1906, W. J. Seymour, who had attended

---

[225] See 1 Corinthians 12:10.

[226] Francis X. Gumerlock, "The Interpretation of Tongues in the Middle Ages," *Antiphon: A Journal for Liturgical Renewal* 10:2 (2006): 160–168.

a Pentecostal school in Houston, went to Los Angeles and began instructing potential converts, first in a Nazarene church, and later in a ramshackle building on Azusa Street. By year's end Pentecostalism claimed 13,000 adherents in the United States and Canada. The Azusa Street revivals engendered the classical Pentecostalism associated with the "Church of God in Christ" and the Assemblies of God, the two largest Pentecostal groups, besides numberless storefront Pentecostal chapels. In the 1960s and 1970s, Pentecostal-like experiences began to be seen in the mainline churches, including the Catholic Church. This was identified as the "charismatic renewal."

A good starting point for assessing the Holiness and Pentecostal accounts of salvation from a Catholic perspective might be our common belief that life in Christ is impossible without the Holy Spirit and incomplete without a special gift of the Spirit. Christians are children of the Father because they have been taken up into the life of Christ's Sonship by the Holy Spirit, the Spirit of adoption.[227] Christian life is to be a maturing into more perfect sonship until we grow into the full stature of Christ.[228] Since it is by the Holy Spirit that our adoption as sons and daughters in Christ is effected, it will be for the same Spirit to perfect that adoption. In the Catholic understanding, birth into Christian life is perfected, not by a special "Baptism in the Spirit" received after water Baptism, but by the Sacrament of Confirmation: the Spirit of adoption, already bestowed in Baptism, comes in a new and abundant manner in Confirmation to complete the baptismal grace of adoption. Pentecost is a unique event in the history of salvation. Even so, in Confirmation the Christian receives the abundant outpouring of the Spirit that in some way reflects and continues the mystery of Pentecost.

The Wesleyan-Holiness emphasis on sanctification and moral transformation accords with the Catholic belief that God not only forgives us but also makes us holy. Wesley believed that, for most Christians, complete sanctification takes place just before death. In other words, the work that Catholics ascribe to Purgatory is, for Wesley, accomplished immediately by a unilateral act of God at death. In another historical circumstance, Wesley

---

[227] See Romans 8:15.
[228] See Ephesians 4:13.

might have accepted the Catholic idea of sanctification after death, for Purgatory seems necessary if God is to complete the job with human freedom intact.

THE MENNONITES AND THE AMISH

Once the Protestant Reformation sundered the unity of Western Christendom, groups on the Reformation's "left" wing urged a complete return to what they considered primitive Christianity. Chief among these radical sects were the various Anabaptist communities, which denied the validity of infant Baptism, re-quiring re-baptism of all who had been baptized as infants. During the most brutal periods of persecution from all sides, Anabaptists sought safety by withdrawing from mainstream society, trying to live simply, piously, and peaceably. In time this became their hallmark and that of their descendants.

The term "Mennonite" refers to a large number of similar but separate groups, all descended from the Anabaptists. These groups take their name from Menno Simons (1496–1561), an ex-Catholic priest from Friesland (a region now shared between Germany and the Netherlands) who organized and institutional-ized the dozens of independent Anabaptist communities. The Mennonites disapproved of violence for any reason, lawsuits, the swearing of oaths, and the holding of public office. They pre-ferred an untrained and unsalaried ministry chosen by lot, and sought to establish a voluntary Church of saints, in contrast to a Church that embraced believers and mere conformists alike. Fail-ure to meet one's moral, religious, and social responsibilities could result in "the ban" or "shunning," by which an unfaithful member is excommunicated, ostracized, and in some cases re-buffed as if he were dead. Disputes over principles of the ban resulted in factions. Today, only the most conservative Menno-nite groups practice the ban.

The first Mennonite congregation in America was founded in 1683 at Germantown, Pennsylvania. Mennonites took their paci-fism seriously, refusing to take up arms in the Revolutionary War. After the war they were accused of treason for feeding starving British soldiers. During the Civil War, when both sides had mandatory conscription, most Mennonites hired substitutes or paid a hefty exemption fee. In the two world wars of the twentieth century, Mennonite men were exempted from military combat in exchange for serving in such positions as clerks or hospital orderlies.

The promise of land and exemption from military conscription lured thousands of German Mennonites to Russia beginning in 1788. They settled there, while retaining their German language and culture. Almost a century later, however, the Tsar required that all Russians, including the pacifist Mennonites, serve in the military. Many Mennonites left for America, settling primarily in the Midwest.

In 1860, representatives of several independent Mennonite groups met in Iowa to form a North American conference, later called the General Conference Mennonite Church. The largest Mennonite body, known simply as the Mennonite Church, merged with the General Conference Mennonite Church in 2002; the united body is called the Mennonite Church USA and numbers 109,000 members among more than 900 congregations. Most of the world's 1.6 million Mennonites live in North America, Africa, India, and Indonesia. A Mennonite World Conference is held every six years, but it is strictly for communication and mutual support. It has no doctrinal or jurisdictional authority over any local conference or congregation.

In the 1690s, a major schism took place. Jacob Amman, the chief elder or "bishop" of Switzerland, left the established Mennonites to form a new community dedicated to strict enforcement of the ban. Amman was influenced by the Lutheran Pietist movement, which emphasized personal religious experience and simplicity of life. For example, the Pietists used hooks and eyes instead of buttons, because buttons at that time were a symbol of status and wealth. Amman and his followers renounced all modern conveniences. Almost all supported themselves by farming. They called themselves Old Order Amish Mennonites, after Amman's name, but are usually simply called Amish. Many Amish migrated to America, most settling in Pennsylvania and the Midwest.

By the beginning of the twentieth century, many Mennonites had become more modern in their approach, dropping their traditional use of German and instituting such mainstream practices as Sunday schools, inter-congregational organizations, and missionary work. This led to a number of divisions, and today there are several Mennonite groups, spanning a wide spectrum. Some, such as the Amish, are easily recognizable by their clothing: the men wear dark trousers, a long-sleeved shirt with a vest, and a straw hat; women wear a "no frills" dress and a small cap or bonnet. Among many Mennonite groups it is the custom that the men are clean-shaven until they marry, and then grow a beard to show their unavailability.

The Amish and Mennonites affirm the core Christian doctrines of the Trinity, Incarnation, and atonement. They look to the Bible as their sole authority for doctrine and primary guide to living. They practice "Believer's Baptism" (never infant Baptism) as a ritual testimony of their faith. Neither Baptism nor Communion is considered a sacrament in the Catholic sense, that is, as a conveyer of God's grace. Communion is held only annually or semi-annually in most congregations and is usually accompanied by the washing of feet, after Jesus' example and command.[229] Amish worship is conducted in homes or barns rather than in churches.

Christians in the Anabaptist tradition are admired for their honesty, simplicity, industriousness, strong sense of community, and witness for peace. Although they are far removed from the liturgical and sacramental core of the living apostolic Tradition, and although one might fault them for seeking to erase the distinction between the Church and her sinful members, their exemplary conduct provides valuable lessons for mainstream Christians, who by definition manifest the least degree of difference from their surrounding culture. Like the ancient Christians with the culture of pagan antiquity, the Amish in particular embrace a radical way of being in the world but not of the world.

THE EVANGELICALS

Outside of Catholicism and Pentecostalism, the largest and most rapidly growing sector of Christianity is that which is broadly designated "evangelical Protestant," or simply "evangelicalism" (usually not capitalized). What the philosopher Wittgenstein

[229] See John 13:1–17.

said about the aroma of coffee can be said likewise of evangelicalism: everyone knows it exists, but no one can precisely describe it. Evangelicalism is not a denominational family, like Presbyterianism or Lutheranism, but an umbrella term used to unite conservative Christians from different traditions. Consequently, the differences among evangelicals are often very stark. For example, some evangelicals affirm Calvinist predestination while others prefer Arminian free will. The fact that many Baptists, Pentecostals, Methodists, Presbyterians, Lutherans, and Anglicans identify themselves as evangelical only adds to the confusion. Although many small evangelical denominations have been formed in the last hundred years, most evangelicals are members of independent, nondenominational congregations with names such as Grace Gospel Church or Calvary Bible Church. What, then, holds the evangelical world together? Where is its center of gravity?

Most observers agree that in addition to affirming traditional Christian doctrines such as the Trinity and the two natures of Christ (human and divine), evangelicals emphasize the inerrancy and authority of the Bible, the necessity of accepting Christ as Lord and Savior (being "born again"), the atoning sacrifice of the Cross, and the importance of bearing witness to the Gospel. "At bottom," explains Catholic convert and writer Thomas Howard, "one cannot distinguish evangelical teaching from traditional Christian orthodoxy. . . . And yet the *flavor* of evangelicalism is very different from that of the traditional Church."[230]

That flavor is defined by a double negative. First, evangelicalism is definitely Protestant, which means that it is neither Catholic nor Orthodox. Absent from evangelical teaching are such doctrines as the Real Presence of Christ in the Eucharist, the sacraments as divinely instituted channels of grace, the apostolic succession of bishops, the authority of Tradition, and the intercession of the saints in glory. Second, evangelicalism is not mainline or liberal Protestant. The mainline churches (Presbyterian, Congregationalist, Episcopalian, and the like) have

---

[230] Thomas Howard, *Evangelical Is Not Enough: Worship of God in Liturgy and Sacrament* (San Francisco: Ignatius Press, 1984), pp. 3, 4.

[231] Nancy Tatom Ammerman, "Golden Rule Christianity: Lived Religion in the American Mainstream," in *Lived Religion in America*, ed. David Hall (Princeton University Press, 1997), pp. 196–216.

largely capitulated to the sexual revolution of the 1960s, espousing what one sociologist terms a "Golden Rule Christianity" that honors tolerance, inclusivity, and social justice (except for preborn children) as paramount virtues.[231] Evangelicals, however, have resisted the abdication of moral principles that Christians have held since the earliest days of the Faith.

"Evangelical" was first used to designate the adherents of the Lutheran Reformation. It was later applied to the early Methodists and others who sought to reinvigorate Christian faith within the Church of England. Evangelicalism is rooted also in Christian fundamentalism, an American movement occurring at the turn of the twentieth century in opposition to liberal trends within Protestantism. Among these trends was a strong skepticism about Christianity's supernatural content—the inspiration of Scripture, the virgin birth and bodily Resurrection of Jesus, miracles, and so forth. While those liberal Protestants who called themselves "modernists" sought to accommodate traditional Christian beliefs to modern science and culture, their conservative opponents were eager "to do battle royal for the fundamentals," in the words of Baptist pastor Curtis Lee Laws. American Protestants fought bitter internal battles over who would control their denominational seminaries, local churches, and mission boards.

The fundamentalists were the cultural losers in the modernist-fundamentalist conflict symbolized by the famous Scopes "monkey trial" of 1925. After their defeat, they became increasingly sectarian, taking refuge in an allegedly pure, literal understanding of the Bible detached from the interpretative Tradition of the wider Christian community. The story of modern evangelicalism began during World War II, when a number of fundamentalist leaders called for reengagement with the culture. The cause of the old fundamentalists who were now the "new evangelicals" was represented by *Christianity Today* magazine and, above all, by the ministry, spanning half a century, of Billy Graham.

Virtually all of the differences between evangelicals and Catholics concern the idea of mediation. The "one Mediator between God and men" is Jesus Christ,[232] present and active in His

---

[232] 1 Timothy 2:5.

mystical Body, the Church. Evangelicals stress the relationship of the individual Christian to God, whereas Catholics accentuate the communal nature of salvation. The Catholic has no reluctance in seeing his relationship with God in Christ being realized through the sacraments, the saints, and a hierarchical ministry, for any mediation attributed to the Church—which includes Mary and the saints—is only part of the mediation of Christ. Evangelicals, on the other hand, tend to regard all these secondary mediators (except for the Bible) as "getting in the way."

A growing chorus of evangelicals is calling for a recovery of the "catholic" roots of the Faith embodied in the great creeds, theology, worship, and spirituality of the early Church.[233] This desire for continuity with the Church in history has led many evangelicals to embrace Catholicism (and, less frequently, Orthodoxy), with its richly textured theological and liturgical life. Conversely, more than a few evangelicals are ex-Catholics. Many Catholics who have not been touched by the words of Scripture in the liturgy or in religious instruction later come to have a true conversion of heart and make a personal commitment to live for Christ. Sometimes this conversion takes place outside the Catholic Church. However, as these "reborn" Christians grow in their knowledge of God's Word and in their love for the Savior, they may someday be drawn back to that life of intimate encounter with Christ in the Eucharist for which there is no earthly parallel.

The whole body of Christ stands ever in need of biblically grounded faith combined with the sources of the living Tradition by which the early Church came to know the meaning and content of Scripture. We might call it "evangelical catholicity."

Defining Christian Faithfulness—A Glance Back

Before moving on, it seems well to recap our exploration of the non-Catholic Christian traditions.

First, we studied the apostolic communities that were part of

---

[233] See, for example, D. H. Williams, *Retrieving the Tradition and Renewing Evangelicalism: A Primer for Suspicious Protestants* (Grand Rapids, Mich.: Wm. B. Eerdmans, 1999). The author is a Baptist minister.

the Catholic Church until the fifth century. Political difficulties, nationalism, and anti-imperial sentiment had as much to do with their separation from the rest of Christendom as theological controversy. The Church of the East, today called the Assyrian Church of the East, broke with the wider Christian communion after the Council of Ephesus (431) declared the Virgin Mary to be the Mother of God. This in response to Nestorius, the bishop of Constantinople (later deposed) who seemed to have held that there were two separate persons in Christ, one divine (the Second Person of the Trinity, God the Son) and the other human (the man Jesus, born of Mary). Consequently, Nestorius thought it was nonsense to say that God was born, suffered, and died. The decree of Ephesus was meant to safeguard the unity of Christ's human and divine natures. The Church of the East sided with Nestorius and went its own way. Nestorianism flourished, first in Syria, then in Persia. Nestorian missionaries even reached parts of distant India and China, and Nestorian Christianity became one of the major religions of Genghis Khan's vast Mongol Empire.

Defining Jesus' identity is a balancing act. If His humanity was separated from His divinity, one committed the heresy of Nestorianism; if it was crowded out by His divinity, one committed the opposite heresy, Monophysitism. In response to the latter, the fourth ecumenical council, held at Chalcedon in 451, proclaimed Christ to have two distinct natures, divine and human, united in the one Divine Person of the Son. A great number of Christians, beginning with the Coptic Church in Egypt, refused to acknowledge the Council of Chalcedon and departed from Catholic unity. These "non-Chalcedonian" churches are collectively named Oriental Orthodox. While being in full communion with one another, each is hierarchically independent.

From the Assyrian and Oriental Orthodox Churches, we turned our attention to the Orthodox Church of the East, a family of self-governing ethnic churches—Russian, Ukrainian, Serbian, Romanian, Greek, and others—held together by a common faith and sacramental life. For nearly a millennium, the Eastern or Byzantine Church, centered on Constantinople, and the Western or Latin Church, centered on Rome, were two parts of a single communion. While the foundations of the Faith were the same, doctrine was expressed differently in East and West. Deep disagreement over papal supremacy, worsened by mutual mistrust and mistreatment, eventually led to the tragic schism in 1054. How "Orthodox" became the proper name of the Eastern Church, it is difficult to say. The name was used at first by the Byzantines, not with any idea of opposition against the Latins, but rather as the antithesis to the Nestorians and Monophysites. Gradually, "Catholic" became the common name for the original Church in the West, "Orthodox" in the East.

The biggest share of our time was spent in Protestantism. It was necessary first to consider the causes and results of the sixteenth-century Reformation. What the Reformation claimed to be espousing was not a new, "Protestant" Gospel but the faith of the true Church, the Catholic Church of all times, as against the false "papal" Church. The Reformers retained a great deal of historic Christianity: Baptism in the name of the Trinity, Christ acknowledged as fully human yet fully divine, the Apostles' and Nicene-Constantinopolitan creeds, and—what is more fundamental—the authoritative use of a collection of texts known as the Bible. However, many Protestants, disconnecting the Bible from the Church's theological heritage and claiming the privilege of private interpretation, soon found it possible to discard infant Baptism, sacraments, Marian doctrine and devotion, and even Trinitarian orthodoxy.

After considering the origins and preoccupations of the chief branches of Protestantism—Lutheran, Reformed, Anglican, Anabaptist—we surveyed the myriad denominational families and their offshoots within the contemporary Protestant world. It is no exaggeration to say that every emphasis spawned its own denomination, each one missing the forest for a few trees. In recent decades, many Protestants have tried to put together again those separate pieces that were pulled apart. The acceptance of grace through faith, the normativity of Scripture, the priesthood of all Christians: these Protestant "distinctives" can form part of the total life and teaching of the one Church. It is a matter of combining them with the Catholic understanding of the Church as both the sacrament of Christ, mediating salvation through institu-

[234] See Peter Kreeft, *Fundamentals of the Faith: Essays in Christian Apologetics* (San Francisco: Ignatius Press, 1988), p. 257.

tional means of grace, and the communion of saints bound to Christ through time. To borrow an analogy, the Church is not a melting pot but a stew in which every ingredient is preserved in the mix of many differences, not melted down.[234]

We may prayerfully hope that a day will come when all who profess faith in the Lord Jesus Christ will live in renewed, visible communion with one another. When the prayer of Jesus in John 17 is fulfilled, there will be but one sheepfold. Only God knows what the institutional form of Christian unity would look like. We can know that it will entail unity in the fullness of the truth that Christ intends for His Church, in Eucharistic celebration, and in communion with the continuing ministry of the Apostles. In a word, it will be *catholic*, embracing the totality of Christian experience and Tradition. Just as orthodoxy is not the private domain of Orthodoxy, so also there are elements of catholicity beyond Catholicism. And yet, as I hope to have demonstrated, the dimensions and structures of catholicity have developed more robustly on the Catholic estate than anywhere else. To come to this realization is to have discerned the whole in the part.

V

CHRISTIANITY'S SPIN-OFFS

IT remains for us to survey the exotic offshoots of Christianity that have arisen in Western societies since the Reformation: Unitarian Universalism, Seventh-day Adventism, Mormonism, Jehovah's Witnesses, and Christian Science. Although historically rooted in Christianity, they stand far from the central Christian tradition and are no more Protestant than Catholic.

Unitarian Universalism

Unitarian Universalism is not so much a religion as a society of "freethinkers" who reject authority and dogma in religious thought. Freedom of belief, enlightened reason, broad and tolerant sympathy, and ethical living are what truly matter. The Unitarian Universalist Association (UUA) was formed in 1961 from the merger of two historically Christian groups: the Unitarians and the Universalists. There are a little more than a thousand UUA congregations in North America and a handful of other similar groups elsewhere that are not officially part of the UUA. Most groups meet on Sunday morning, not for any religious reason, but simply for the sake of tradition and convenience. The loosely structured service centers on a presentation by a minister, lay leader, or invited speaker. Rarely is prayer offered or the word "God" mentioned. Because Unitarian Universalists recognize no single body of texts as divinely revealed, they draw inspiration from many different belief systems: Judaism and Christianity, but also Eastern religions, New Age fashions, and more. Many congregations celebrate observances associated with other religious traditions, including Buddhist-style meditation and Passover Seders.

How did this eclectic "religion" come about? It has been wisely said that there are no new heresies, only warmed-over old ones.

Without any reference to the Church's living and developed Tradition to guide the interpretation of Scripture, believers become highly susceptible to repeating old heresies. In the sixteenth century a Spaniard named Miguel Serveto, better known in the Latinized form Servetus, denounced the doctrine of the Trinity as "the product of subtlety and madness." He tried unsuccessfully to win the Reformers to his Unitarian position, which was of course rehashed Arianism. Luther and Calvin held that non-biblical terms such as "Trinity" and "consubstantial" were not necessary to Christian language, although both men held absolutely to the ideas expressed by those terms. It seems that Calvin slyly denounced Servetus to the Catholic Inquisition. Servetus managed to escape from a Catholic prison in France. On his way, perhaps, to northern Italy in October 1553, he crossed the border to Geneva, probably at Calvin's invitation. There he was arrested, tried, and burned at the stake for blasphemy by Protestant authorities.

Although Servetus attracted no great following, Unitarianism took root in Poland under the influence of the Italian-born Anabaptist Fausto Sozzini (after whose Latinized name of Socinus the Unitarians would later be generally known) and in Transylvania (today a part of Romania) under the leadership of Francis David. The Jesuits eradicated Unitarianism in Poland. In Transylvania, however, Unitarians enjoyed the protection of King John Sigismund, a disciple of David and self-proclaimed Unitarian. After the king's death, persecution by Sigismund's successors forced the Transylvanian Unitarians to go underground.

An ex-Anglican clergyman, Theophilus Lindsey, founded English Unitarianism. Lindsey was aided by Joseph Priestley, the scientist who discovered oxygen. Although Unitarianism in England was not subjected to the severe persecution it endured on the continent, it did antagonize orthodox-minded Christians. In 1791, a mob destroyed Priestley's home as well as a Unitarian chapel in Birmingham. Priestley fled to London and a few years later to America, where he founded a congregation in Northumberland, Pennsylvania.

Unitarianism in New England originated as a rebellion against Calvinist Congregationalism. Unlike Calvinists, Unitarians believed that human nature was essentially good, that God predestined nobody to damnation, and that Jesus was a great moral teacher but not a divine person. The growing controversy was brought to a head by Jedidiah Morse, an orthodox Congregationalist and the father of the inventor of the telegraph. Morse launched a crusade to smoke out the heretics and found a perfect issue when Harvard, Congregationalism's primary training ground for clergymen, appointed a Unitarian to head its divinity school in 1805. In protest, Morse and other conservatives founded Andover Theological Seminary. Most Congregational churches in the Boston area became Unitarian, and in 1825 a group of New England ministers formed the American Unitarian Association.

Meanwhile, Universalism was establishing roots in this country. John Murray, a former Methodist, preached the first Universalist sermon in America in 1770. Originally Universalism was Trinitarian but, like Unitarianism, moved to a point where it was no longer Christian in any particular sense. Universalism is the doctrine that everyone will ultimately be saved and Hell abolished. One of its notable representatives was the third-century theologian Origen of Alexandria (*ca.* 185–254), who taught that at the end of time all creatures, including the Devil, might come to salvation. Three centuries after Origen's death, the Church declared this view heretical.[235] What Hell is like—aside from being horrible indeed—and who, if anyone, is "there"—these and other questions are subject to thoughtful disagreements. But who we are and how we live have *eternal* consequences, for better or for worse.

Unitarian Universalism presents itself as a home for secular humanists, atheists, agnostics, and the "spiritual but not religious" crowd. Its openness to diverse ways of believing and thinking is part, but only a part, of what being "catholic" means. The rest has to do with identity and commitment. As the ever-witty Chesterton said, "The object of opening the mind, as of opening the mouth, is to shut it again on something solid."[236]

---

[235] The doctrine was formally condemned in the first of the famous anathemas pronounced at the provincial Council of Constantinople in 543.

[236] *The Autobiography of G. K. Chesterton*, ed. Randall Paine (San Francisco: Ignatius Press, 2006), p. 217.

Seventh-day Adventism

Seventh-day Adventism dates from the nineteenth-century enthusiasm for predicting the Second Coming of Christ. William Miller (1782–1849), a Baptist farmer in upstate New York, spearheaded the American version. From his reading of Bible prophecy, Miller calculated that Christ would return in 1843–44 to cleanse "the sanctuary,"[237] which he interpreted as the earth (or the Church). When that period had elapsed, Miller endorsed the position of a group of his followers known as the "seventh-month movement," who claimed Christ would return on October 22, 1844, in the seventh month of the Jewish calendar. The sun rose on the morning of October 23, 1844, as on any other day.

After the "Great Disappointment," most of Miller's followers broke up into factions; the rest either returned to their denominational homes or abandoned religion altogether. A tiny band of diehards theorized that Miller had misidentified the sanctuary: it was not the earth, but the heavenly Holy of Holies, prefigured by the inner sanctuary of the Jerusalem Temple.[238] Instead of descending to earth, in 1844 Christ entered the "true tabernacle in Heaven" to plead His blood in behalf of sinners. Another group of Millerites contended that Christians should observe the Jewish Sabbath—Saturday, the seventh day—instead of Sunday.

These two streams of thought—Christ entering the heavenly tabernacle and the need to keep the Saturday Sabbath—were combined by Ellen Gould White (1827–1915), leader of the Millerite remnant which formed the nucleus of the Seventh-day Adventist Church (SDA). White's purportedly inspired writings are understandably anti-Catholic, for it was the Catholic Church that instituted the Sunday Sabbath. In *The Great Controversy*, first published in 1858 and later expanded, White identifies the Church of Rome as the Whore of Babylon described in chapters 17 and 18 of the Book of Revelation, the popes as antichrists, and Sunday worship as the "mark of the beast."

Organized in 1863 in Battle Creek, Michigan, the SDA counts 15 million members worldwide (about one million in the United States). Adventists have formed a distinctive subculture, accom-

[237] See Daniel 8:14.
[238] See Hebrews 8:5.

plished by an extensive parochial school system and careful Saturday observance. They use a valid form of Baptism, believe in the Trinity and Christ's divinity, and uphold the central Protestant doctrines of "Scripture alone" and justification "by faith alone." In addition, they abstain from alcohol and tobacco. For these reasons, Adventists seem at first glance to be conservative Protestants who stress the Second Coming and attend church on Saturday instead of Sunday. Yet closer examination reveals significant departures from the consensus of Christian thought.

The Third Commandment obliges us to refrain from unnecessary labor and to give God public worship every seventh day, in commemoration of God's rest on the seventh day of creation.[239] So, why was the Christian obligation transferred from Saturday to Sunday? First, because many Jewish converts thought they had still to keep the ceremonial law of Moses, such as circumcision, abstinence from certain meats, and scrupulous observance of Jewish sacrifice on the Sabbath. Saint Paul, in Galatians and Second Corinthians especially, insists that Christians need not observe the rites of the old covenant. (Incidentally, Adventists shun pork and other foods proscribed as "unclean" in Leviticus.) Second, Gentile converts gathered on the first day of the week—Sunday, the day of the Resurrection—to celebrate the Eucharist.[240] With the disappearance of the Jewish Christian churches, Sunday was exclusively observed as the Lord's Day.

Seventh-day Adventists believe that at death the soul enters a state of unconsciousness until the Second Coming, when the saved will be raised incorruptible.[241] The damned will be resurrected one thousand years later at the close of Christ's millennial reign on earth[242] and annihilated by fire. Catholic tradition and the majority Christian position in general, including that of the Protestant Reformers, holds that the millennium is not a literal thousand years, but the entire period between the Incarnation and Second Coming. At Christ's return occur the Last Judgment and the resurrection of the dead, when body and soul are

---

[239] See Exodus 20:8–11.
[240] See Acts 20:7; 1 Corinthians 16:1–2.
[241] See 1 Corinthians 15:42–50; Philippians 3:21.
[242] See Revelation 20.

reunited, with special characteristics of glory for the saints and unending torment in soul and body for the damned.[243]

But where are the dead *now*? "In the grave, asleep and unconscious, until the resurrection," answers the Adventist. A few Old Testament passages suggest this; for example, Psalm 115:17 and Ecclesiastes 9:5.[244] In the New Testament, the idea that the saints are with Christ even before the resurrection is undeveloped. This is partly because of the expectation that Christ would soon return, and partly because Jews and early Christians were rightly concerned that the whole person, body and soul, should be with God. Moreover, some Fathers of the Church, notably Saint Justin Martyr, seem to have held that the souls of the just enter Heaven only after the general judgment and resurrection.

Yet the New Testament already contains, especially in the writings of Saint Paul, the principle from which flow the truths later to be solemnly declared by the Catholic Church: that Heaven, meaning the intuitive vision and loving enjoyment of God, begins even before the resurrection, as soon as the soul is completely purified of sin and its effects;[245] and that Hell, meaning definitive separation from God for those who die in mortal sin unrepentant, begins immediately after death. These truths are latent in the central New Testament idea that the "end times" have already begun. Life and death after Christ's Resurrection are no longer moments in a temporal sequence. In John 5:24, Jesus says that eternal life is a *present* reality for believers. He who lives outside Christ, though he be alive, is dead,[246] while he who dies in Christ, though he be dead, lives.[247]

Mormonism

More than 14 million people, including five million Americans, belong to the Church of Jesus Christ of Latter-day Saints (LDS),

---

[243] See, among others, Matthew 8:12; 10:28 (possibly); 25:46.

[244] Psalm 115:17: "The dead do not praise the Lord, nor do any that go down into silence." Ecclesiastes 9:5: "For the living know that they will die, but the dead know nothing, and they have no more reward; but the memory of them is lost."

[245] That the Beatific Vision is enjoyed by the souls of the just having no faults to expiate is a dogma of Catholic faith, expressly defined by Pope Benedict XII in the Bull *Benedictus Deus* (January 29, 1336).

[246] See 1 Timothy 5:6.

[247] See John 11:25–26.

otherwise known as the Mormon Church. Preponderant in Utah and strong in other western states, the LDS has grown to become the fourth-largest denomination in the United States, largely because of its aggressive missionary program and its high birthrate.

Mormonism's founding stories and doctrines germinated in upstate New York in the early nineteenth century, where new religious sects produced a rainforest of novel revelations. Much of the teaching reflects the liberal Protestantism of the time: belief in continuing revelation, denial of original sin, and unbridled optimism about human perfectibility. Mix that in with the Bible and other scriptures held to be divinely revealed, and the result is Mormonism.

The *Book of Mormon*, which for Mormons is equal in authority to the Bible, proclaims itself "another testament of Jesus Christ." Indeed it is, for it purports to give us another history of what Our Lord said and did—not one to replace the witness of the New Testament, but to supplement it. This third testament contains the stories of Christ's visits, soon after His Ascension, to the Nephites, a branch of the House of Israel, which came to the Americas around 600 B.C., just prior to the Babylonian captivity. In A.D. 421, the other of the two major Book of Mormon peoples, the Lamanites, defeated the Nephites in battle near present-day Palmyra, New York. Mormon, the vanquished Nephite general, had inscribed the history of his people on golden plates, which his son Moroni buried for safekeeping.

According to official Mormon history, Moroni returned in 1823 as an angel and visited Joseph Smith (1805–1844), the son of a Vermont farmer. Some time earlier, the Smith family had relocated to the Finger Lakes region of New York State. When Joseph was fourteen he was visited by God the Father and Jesus, who told him that all existing churches were false and he was to reestablish the true Church. In 1827, at the angel Moroni's behest, he dug near the crest of a hill near Palmyra and unearthed the golden plates. With them were the Urim and Thummin, flat "seer" stones used as a divine oracle, like those described in the Old Testament.[248] Four years later Joseph took possession of the plates and, using the stones, deciphered the inscriptions

---

[248] See, among others, Exodus 28:30, Numbers 27:21, and 1 Samuel 28:6.

from a previous unknown language described as "Reformed Egyptian." The result was the Book of Mormon, published at Palmyra in 1830.

The Book of Mormon contains many verbatim passages from the New Testament but also much that is alien to historic Christianity. It relates that Jesus visited the Nephites and taught them something very close to the King James Version of the Sermon on the Mount, healed their sick, raised the dead, administered Communion with bread and wine, and commissioned twelve native apostles.

Another significant moment in Mormonism's development was in 1829 when Joseph Smith reported that John the Baptist had appeared to him and his scribe and ordained them to the Aaronic or Old Testament priesthood. They also claimed to have been visited by the Apostles Peter, James, and John, who conferred on them the higher priesthood of Melchizedek.

With this higher calling, Smith founded the LDS on April 6, 1830, at Fayette, New York. He wrote down further revelations from Jesus, which form a major part of Mormon doctrine today: the *Doctrine and Covenants* and the *Pearl of Great Price*. Mormons progressed westward to Ohio, where they built a temple at Kirtland and chose twelve apostles as Smith's assistants. Some Mormons went to England as missionaries. Others continued to Missouri, where they entered into conflict with the old settlers and eventually were expelled.

Most observers were suspicious of Mormonism, especially with its exclusive claims and secret rituals, but especially because of rumors of polygamy—always a controversial subject for Mormons. (Smith had no fewer than thirty wives.) The legitimacy of polygamy was allegedly revealed to Smith in 1843, but it was only after the largest group of Mormons settled in Utah that polygamy was openly practiced. Under government pressure, the LDS finally gave it up in 1890. Today the LDS does not endorse polygamy, although smaller breakaway sects continue the practice.

Because of this and other controversies, Smith was jailed numerous times, as well as tarred and feathered. On June 27, 1844, while awaiting trial in Carthage, Illinois, he and his brother Hyrum were shot to death by a mob. The LDS was left without a defined leader. Eventually one did emerge: Brigham Young (1801–1877), Smith's longtime supporter and fellow Vermonter. In 1846, Young led many of the Mormons on a harsh trek westward in order "to get away from Christians and out of the United States." Survivors of the perilous journey reached the valley of the Great Salt Lake (then a part of Mexico) in 1847 and established a permanent community, bringing a rich harvest from what was barren desert.

Not all LDS members accepted Young's leadership. The largest of these splinter groups eventually became the Reorganized Church of Jesus Christ of Latter-day Saints with headquarters near Independence, Missouri. While much smaller than the LDS (only 250,000 members), this group disavows some of Smith's more esoteric doctrines and is today practically indistinguishable from any mainline Protestant denomination. In 2001 they were renamed the Community of Christ.

LDS headquarters is in Salt Lake City, Utah. At the top of the church hierarchy is the First Presidency, composed of the President (who is also prophet, seer, and revelator) and his two counselors, claiming powers that would have made Saint Peter blush. The Quorum of the Twelve Apostles elects the President for life and acts under the direction of the First Presidency. Local LDS congregations are called wards and are headed by "bishops" who usually hold secular jobs. Wards are grouped into stakes governed by stake presidents.

Children are baptized at age eight. From age twelve every Mormon male (including, since 1978, blacks) is eligible for membership in the Aaronic and Melchizedek priesthoods. The former includes the office of deacon and is concerned with forming good Christians, while the latter is involved with officiating in the church.

Proxies are baptized on behalf of the dead, and families hope to go on living together and procreating in a celestial eternity. Sunday worship includes readings, prayer, teaching, and communion of blessed bread and water (Mormons abstain from alcohol). Beyond the ward, many Mormons engage in esoteric temple rites similar to early Masonic rituals.

A substantial number of Christians believe that Mormons are not Christians. One reason is that Latter-day Saints regard the

Book of Mormon as God's Word, on a par with the Bible. It is the certain teaching of the Catholic Church and most other Christian communions that Divine Revelation ended with the death of the last Apostle, even if our understanding and application of God's Word did not. For roughly the first four Christian centuries, debate persisted about what writings did or did not belong in the Bible. Christians eventually came to agree that 27 books form the New Testament. As to what constitutes the Old Testament, disagreement remains, with Protestants subscribing only to those books that for Jews now go under the name of the Hebrew Bible, while Catholics and Orthodox additionally admit certain Jewish texts that were written in Greek or survived only in Greek translation. In those controversies, the word used to describe the books that made it into the Bible was "canon," from the Greek word for "rule" or "measure." In 1546 the Council of Trent defined the biblical canon, thereby excluding for Catholics the possibility that there could be any inspired Scripture beyond the Bible. Trent's decision was based on the decrees of previous councils and popes, and longstanding liturgical practice.

The preceding historical note illustrates that the determination of what is Scripture is grounded in the Church's living Tradition of faith, even as Tradition is itself grounded in Scripture. Unlike the Bible, the Book of Mormon is not a product of the living faith of Israel and the Apostles. For starters, not a single person, place, or event that is unique to the Book of Mormon has ever been proven to exist. While the canonical Gospels and other voices testify to the Jesus of the New Testament, the only voice testifying to the authenticity of the Jesus of the Book of Mormon is Joseph Smith. Then there are the inconsistencies, too many to catalog here, between the biblical Jesus and the Jesus of the Book of Mormon, and further discrepancies between the Jesus of the Book of Mormon and the Jesus of later Joseph Smith prophecies.

Which brings us to another basic difference between Mormonism and traditional Christianity: the nature of God. Several times

---

[249] LDS Church Apostle Bruce R. McConkie (1915–1985), in his 1958 book *Mormon Doctrine: A Compendium of the Gospel*, draws a distinction between the Holy Ghost and the Holy Spirit. The Holy Ghost is "a Personage of Spirit, a Spirit Person, a Spirit Man" (p. 359), while the Holy Spirit is an impersonal, purely spiritual

the Book of Mormon refers to the Father, Son, and Holy Ghost[249] as "one God," but Latter-day Saints understand this to mean they are one in mind and purpose rather than one indivisible being. For this reason, they seldom use the word "Trinity," but prefer the term "Godhead" to refer to the three divine beings who govern our universe. This is tri-theism, not Trinitarianism.

Drawing from Smith's later teachings, Mormons believe that the Father is an exalted man with flesh and bones who attained Godhood after His own death as a human. The Son, prior to His embodied life on earth, was the Father's firstborn spirit-child who created this world at the Father's direction. The Holy Ghost is purely spiritual but looks like a man. Jesus was born of the Virgin Mary and atoned for the sins of mankind on the Cross. At His Resurrection, He assumed an immortal, glorified body like that of the Father. As a man, He gradually accumulated the divine nature; thus He is at the end of the progression along which we too can proceed by exercising Christian faith.

By contrast, orthodox Christian tradition holds that the three Divine Persons are neither separate deities (for God is perfect unity) nor parts of the Godhead (for God is indivisible), but one eternal God. Moreover, instead of becoming divine, Christ always was divine. The eternal Son voluntarily and humbly "emptied Himself" of some of His divine prerogatives by becoming man, but this was merely a camouflaging of the fullness of divinity.[250] The Mormon belief that humans can progress toward divinity is in some ways an undigested version of the great formula of the Church Fathers, "God became man that man might become God." In short, to be saved is to be divinized in Christ by the Holy Spirit; still, the distinction between Creator and creature forever remains.

In sum, Mormonism radically departs from historic Christianity as defined by Scripture and the creeds of the ancient Church, but neither is it explicable apart from Christianity. Mormons use

---

essence or force--likened to electricity—employed by the Holy Ghost to accomplish His purposes. McConkie's compendium served as a standard reference for Mormons for more than fifty years. It was revised in 1966 to clarify points of doctrine and modify its tone, and again revised in 1978 after the "revelation" that all races are eligible for priesthood.

[250] See Philippians 2:7–8; Colossians 1:19, 2:9.

traditional Christian vocabulary but mean something very different. For this reason, many Christians maintain that the LDS is not a Christian denomination. The Catholic Church does not recognize the validity of Mormon baptism.[251]

Jehovah's Witnesses

With a worldwide membership exceeding seven million (one million in the United States), the religion known as Jehovah's Witnesses traces its origin to Charles Taze Russell (1852–1916), the son of a Pittsburgh haberdasher. Raised a Presbyterian, Russell became an agnostic at age seventeen but later embraced Adventist and occultist beliefs. In 1881 he founded Zion's Watch Tower Tract Society as an unincorporated administrative agency for the purpose of disseminating Bibles and religious tracts. A few years later, the society was legally incorporated in Pennsylvania and officially renamed the Watch Tower Bible and Tract Society. Russell laid out his fundamental doctrines in a six-volume series called *Millennial Dawn*, later renamed *Studies in the Scriptures*. By 1909, the work had become international and the society's headquarters were moved to its present location in Brooklyn, New York.

"Judge" Joseph F. Rutherford (1869–1942), a Missouri lawyer and former Baptist, succeeded Russell as president. Rutherford's early presidency was marked by bitter disputes with the board of directors, prompting many defections from the organization. He imposed a centralized administrative structure which he called "Theocratic Government," introduced doctrinal revisions, and expected every member to devote many hours a month to door-to-door visitations. In 1931, the society adopted the name "Jehovah's Witnesses."

Why "Jehovah"? Early written Hebrew had no vowels. God's name was written "JHVH" (probably pronounced *YAH-way*).[252] Out of reverence, its use was avoided. When the Scriptures were read, the reader said instead *Adonai*, "my Lord." When vowels were inserted into the Hebrew text, the vowels of "Adonai" were

---

[251] Congregation for the Doctrine of the Faith, *Responsum ad propositum dubium* (On the question of baptism conferred in the Church of Jesus Christ of Latter-day Saints), dated June 5, 2001, in *Acta Apostolicae Sedis* 93 (2001): 476.

[252] Exodus 3:14.

added to "JHVH," producing a hybrid that was introduced into English as "Jehovah."

Because Jehovah's Witnesses grew out of the nineteenth-century Adventist tradition, its emphasis is on the end times. Russell taught that Christ would return to earth in 1914. When that year had come and gone, he claimed that Christ had indeed returned in 1914, but that His return was invisible. When He finally returns physically, the final conflict between good and evil, the battle of Armageddon will take place.[253] Christ will triumph and set up His earthly thousand-year kingdom. During that period, people will be resurrected and given a second chance to receive salvation by accepting the Gospel. Then Satan and his demons will be released for a short time, after which they and their human followers will be annihilated.

Following a literal interpretation of the number mentioned in Revelation 7:4 and 14:1, Witnesses believe that after the final battle exactly 144,000 will go to Heaven and reign with Christ. Those belonging to this "anointed class" will not have resurrected bodies, but "spirit-bodies." The "other sheep" who survive Armageddon will live forever in resurrected bodies on a recreated Paradise Earth.

Rutherford declared that Christ's visible return would occur during the lifetime of "millions" of people alive in 1914. Having predicted the end times for 1914, 1918, 1925, 1941, and 1975, the Watchtower Society has learned from experience not to specify dates. It is enough to observe that relatively very few people today were alive in 1914, and their numbers are fast dwindling.

The most important religious service of the year is the Memorial of Christ's Death, which takes place on the anniversary of the Last Supper, calculated according to the lunar calendar in use in Christ's time. Those only who believe themselves to be anointed partake of the bread and wine at the annual Memorial in local Kingdom Halls.

Satan is marshaling his forces for Armageddon, and his principal allies are the churches and political organizations. Witnesses regard all public institutions as Satan's instruments; hence, they do not vote in local or national elections, hold public office, salute

---

[253] See Revelation 16:16.

the flag, join civic associations and lodges, or volunteer for military service. (During World War I, Rutherford and his associates spent nine months in prison on charges of sedition for refusing to serve in the military.) They do not celebrate Christmas or Easter because these festivals have pagan origins; nor do they celebrate birthdays or other secular festivals. They interpret the biblical prohibition of ingesting blood [254] as including blood transfusions, even in cases of medical emergency. Praying with non-Witnesses ("Gentiles") is a grievous offense.

Witnesses reject the fundamental Christian doctrines of the divinity of Christ, His bodily Resurrection, and the Trinity. Their Christology puts a new spin on the ancient Arian heresy. Christ is not God but a created intermediary, the firstborn of creation,[255] who lived in Heaven as a "spirit-being" before He appeared on earth. In His pre-human state He was Michael the Archangel, an identification that relies on a fanciful linking of the Letter of Jude, verse 9, with First Thessalonians 4:16.[256] Upon coming to earth He ceased to be angelic and was purely human. After His execution on a single upright stake (not a cross), what was resurrected was Michael's glorified spirit. Moreover, the Holy Spirit is not a Divine Person, but God's active power.

Like all notable heresies in Christian history, Witnesses appeal earnestly to the authority of Scripture without reference to the Tradition of Christian faith extending from the apostolic era to the present. Worse, they attempt to substantiate their beliefs using their own highly inaccurate translation of the Bible called the New World Translation (NWT). In many places the NWT is unfaithful to the Hebrew and Greek, especially where the text fails to support and often openly contradicts Witnesses' peculiar doctrines. For instance, it renders John 1:1, "In the beginning the Word was, and the Word was with God, and the Word was *a god.*"

---

[254] See Genesis 9:4; Leviticus 17:10, 14; Acts 15:29.

[255] See Colossians 1:15.

[256] Jude 9: "But when the archangel Michael, contending with the devil, disputed about the body of Moses, he did not presume to pronounce a reviling judgment upon him, but said, 'The Lord rebuke you.'" 1 Thessalonians 4:16: "For the Lord himself will descend from heaven with a cry of command, with the archangel's call, and with the sound of the trumpet of God. And the dead in Christ will rise first . . ."

It is one thing to reject historic Christianity as a corruption of the pure Gospel. It is quite another to rewrite Scripture to accommodate heresies old and new.

Christian Science

The last of the spin-offs of historic Christianity to be considered is also the final stop on our tour of world religions: Christian Science. The Church of Christ, Scientist, was founded by Mary Baker Eddy (1821–1910) on the premise that the material world, with all its suffering, strife, and death, is an illusion: God is Spirit, and therefore everything is spirit.

Born Mary Morse Baker in Bow, New Hampshire, she spent her childhood plagued by illness and fits. Though reared in a devout Congregationalist family, her religious thinking drew less from Calvinism than from the enthusiasms of the day: Transcendentalism, Spiritualism, and Mormonism.

In 1843, Miss Baker married George Washington Glover, a building contractor, and moved with him to the Carolinas. She became pregnant, but George died of yellow fever a few months later. She returned to New Hampshire and gave birth to her only child, a son who received his father's name. She found shelter for herself and the boy in her parents' home until her mother's death in late 1849. In 1850, still suffering from recurring bouts of illness and no longer having her mother's help, she had no choice but to place young George in the care of the family's former nurse and her husband, who took the boy with them to Minnesota.

The widow Glover married Daniel Patterson, an itinerant dentist and philanderer, in 1853. Struggling with poor health compounded by personal loss and financial setbacks, she plunged into a deep depression. In 1862, as the Civil War raged, Daniel was captured while sightseeing on a battlefield and spent several months in a Confederate prison. He escaped and eventually took up practice in Lynn, Massachusetts, where his wife rejoined him in 1864.

The year 1866 signaled a crucial turning point in Eddy's life, and not only because Daniel ran off with another woman that summer. In February, she slipped on an icy sidewalk in Lynn and suffered a paralyzing spinal injury. While bedridden, she read the Gospel passage in which Jesus addressed the paralytic: "Rise, take up your bed and go home."[257] Two days later, to the astonishment of friends, she got up unaided. The "fall in Lynn," she later wrote, led her to discover "the Science of Metaphysical Healing," or Christian Science.

According to Eddy, Jesus taught people the power of the mind to eliminate sin, sickness, and death. She recorded these spiritual principles as she had discerned them in her textbook, *Science and Health*, first published in 1875. An 1884 edition included for the first time an allegorical interpretation of Genesis and Revelation boldly styled "Key to the Scriptures." Eddy claimed that *Science and Health* was dictated to her directly by God. An article in the *New York Times* of July 10, 1904 (available to us on the newspaper's website) alleges that she plagiarized the work of Phineas P. Quimby, a popular healer from Maine.

In 1862, then-Mrs. Patterson sought help from Quimby and was cured for a short time, after which her health tended to fluctuate. She returned to him several times the following year, not only for treatment but also to study his method. From Quimby she learned that infirmity was merely an error of mortal mind, and that one could control another's mind without that person's consent or perhaps knowledge.

Disappointed that existing churches ignored Christian Science, Eddy established the Church of Christ, Scientist, in 1879. Its mission was "to reinstate primitive Christianity and its lost element of healing." In 1882, she transferred her activities from Lynn to Boston. Christian Science soon prospered with branch societies in the East and Midwest.

All the while, Eddy suffered in dread of what she called Malicious Animal Magnetism (MAM) and publicly denounced the MAM campaigns waged against her. She accused her enemies of mentally working havoc on her movement even to the point of murdering her third husband, Asa Gilbert Eddy (married 1877; died 1882), with mental arsenic. In 1889 she moved to New Hampshire and dissolved the government of the Boston church. Three years later, she reorganized the church in Boston as the First Church of Christ, Scientist, also known as the Mother

[257] Matthew 9:6

Church. Thereafter all power rested in the Mother Church; all other churches were simply branches, their "pastors" being the Bible and *Science and Health*.

Pneumonia ended Mrs. Eddy's life on December 3, 1910. The sect she founded has little in common with orthodox Christianity. Like Mormonism, it uses Christian vocabulary but assigns different meanings to the terms. God is infinite Mind, and mind is all (shades of Hinduism). The Trinity is Life, Truth, and Love (evocative of Taoism: God's attributes are identified with the divine nature). Salvation is happiness here and now. Jesus is the exemplar of the divine goodness in everyone.

Christian Scientists do not seek conventional medical treatment. The church does not baptize, ordain clergy, or tabulate membership. Its standardized Sunday service consists mainly of readings from the Bible and *Science and Health*.

The grain of truth in Christian Science is that God does not positively will infirmity or other disorders because this would be in flagrant contradiction to His goodness. In the New Testament, the curing of diseases is always associated with the advancement of God's Kingdom. More than a deliverance from sickness and death, however, the establishment of the Kingdom is the redemption of the whole universe,[258] when God's truth, freedom, and the glory of His love will transfigure everything. This recreation can come about only through the reconciliation of all things to the exalted Christ,[259] who truly "suffered in the flesh" [260] and died a real death to atone for real sins.

---

[258] See Romans 8:22.
[259] See Colossians 1:20; Ephesians 1:10.
[260] 1 Peter 4:1.

Afterword

W E have reached the end of our tour, the purpose of which went beyond simply describing the beliefs and practices of other religions and other Christian traditions. Any number of books and websites can serve that purpose. Our purpose was to appreciate Catholicism as the fullness of truth. It would not do simply to indicate where, in the Catholic view, other religious traditions "go wrong." It was necessary also to identify what is true and good in those traditions, and then point to their fulfillment in the Catholic Church.

For instance: In Hinduism, we discovered the "you are That" (*tat tvam asi*) of the Upanishads—roughly speaking, the identity of the Self with God. This Self is not the self of everyday consciousness, or what we mean by "I" (that is an illusion, says the Hindu), but rather the innermost Self, *Atman*, which is *Brahman*, the Universal Soul, the only reality. In addition to what has already been said about this Hindu doctrine in relation to biblical faith, a further observation can be made.

The identification of the individual soul with the ultimate principle of things seems, on the face of it, like self-divinization. Yet it can also work in the reverse, as a preamble to faith in the living God. For the only true self is the one that is received from God in every moment. Nor can the gift be recognized as *gift* without some degree of faith in a Giver. The truth of the Atman-Brahman concept, it would seem, lies in the refusal to construct a false self—such that, for example, I seem to myself to exist at the center of the universe, capable of defining for myself what is real and true—and in the associated refusal to invent a Giver who has not (yet) revealed Himself. The danger, however, lies in a premature ruling out of the possibility that a Giver might still reveal Himself, which is exactly what some forms of Eastern religion have done.[261]

---

[261] The qualifier "some" is necessary because none of the Eastern traditions is homogeneous. Hinduism, for example, admits of profound devotional theism (*Madhva*) but also an austere philosophical monism with elements of devotionalism (*Sankara*).

Let us follow this line of thought as regards Judaism and Islam. Both religions profess faith in a personal God who seeks to establish a relationship with man. For Jews and Muslims, God's perfect unity excludes the possibility of eternal relations within the Godhead, just as God's transcendence or "otherness" precludes His living a human existence. Since God cannot conceivably be a trinity (or, for that matter, a "binity"), His fatherhood is simply a metaphor, a way of speaking about God's relationships to the human family or, more narrowly, to the children of Abraham. For Christians, however, God's fatherhood is more than metaphorical: it is a feature of God's *interior* life—as is sonship, and likewise the union of the two. The Father and Son eternally loving each other in the Holy Spirit is what it means to *be* God. Only the doctrine of the Trinity as affirmed by orthodox Christianity reveals the full dimensions of the truth that God *is* love.[262]

As for the myriad unorthodox Christianities, they are but so many examples of the problem Chesterton described when he wrote: "The idea of birth through a Holy Spirit, of the death of a divine being, of the forgiveness of sins, or the fulfillment of prophecies, are ideas which, any one can see, need but a touch to turn them into something blasphemous or ferocious."[263] Whatever the differences among the sects, they all have one thing in common: a strong attachment to one theme or one portion of the Christian revelation, which they have never learned to balance and integrate with the rest. But fragmentary Christianity, especially where it rests on the principle of private judgment in matters of faith and morals, cannot be relied upon for the truth that makes us free.[264] The only sure foundation of Christian hope is the entire Christian revelation—the fullness of truth.

Even as we who are Catholic believe that Christianity is the fullest revelation of God and Catholicism its profoundest expression, we must say this with humility. We do not know and live out that fullness ourselves. As Saint Paul said, each of us grasps only fragmentary aspects of the Truth we hope to encounter fully

---

[262] See 1 John 4:8.
[263] G. K. Chesterton, *Orthodoxy* (1908; repr. San Francisco: Ignatius Press, 1995), p. 106.
[264] See John 8:32.

in eternity.[265] What we will be in eternity begins on this side of death. The Buddhist who is moved to compassion by the teaching of the Buddha; the Muslim who strives to live an upright life through prayer, almsgiving, and fasting; the Jew who lives by faith in the God of Abraham, Isaac, Jacob, and Jesus—each is demonstrating obedience to an impulse of grace. This is not to suggest that all religions mediate salvation to a greater or lesser extent. Grace comes always by means of Christ in the Holy Spirit through the mediation of the Church which is Christ's mystical Body and the Temple of His Spirit—albeit often in ways known to God alone. That noted, it is possible to discern the touches of God's Spirit in other religions without ignoring or glossing over what is false and unholy in them.

God wills that all people embrace the fullness of Christ in the Catholic Church where alone that fullness is found. It is a betrayal of Christ to neglect or oppose the preaching of the Gospel to non-Christians on the ground that they already know God, implicitly at least, according to their own lights. It is likewise a betrayal to cease calling our separated Christian brothers and sisters to visible unity with the successor of Saint Peter on the ground that their communities possess, in varying degrees, authentic "ecclesial" elements of sanctification and truth. Much will be required of those to whom much has been entrusted, Jesus promised.[266] Given the riches with which we Catholics have been blessed—the Deposit of Faith in its entirety, the teaching authority given by Christ and guided by the Holy Spirit, and, above all, the inestimable gift of the Eucharist—and despite how unmoved by these gifts we sometimes are, it may be that, in the fullness of God's mercy, we too can be saved.

---

[265] See 1 Corinthians 13:12.
[266] See Luke 12:48.

FOR FURTHER READING

Among the numerous sources I consulted in the writing of this book are the following works of a more general nature:

Clark, Francis. *Godfaring: On Reason, Faith, and Sacred Being.* Washington, D.C.: The Catholic University of America Press, 2000.

Copleston, Frederick. *Religion and the One: Philosophies East and West.* London: Search Press, 1982.

D'Costa, Gavin. *Christianity and World Religions: Disputed Questions in the Theology of Religions.* Chichester, Eng.: Wiley-Blackwell, 2009.

———. *The Meeting of Religions and the Trinity.* Faith Meets Faith Series. Maryknoll, N.Y.: Orbis Books, 2000.

Kereszty, Roch A. *Christianity among Other Religions: Apologetics in a Contemporary Context.* Edited by Andrew C. Gregg. New York: Alba House, 2006.

Ratzinger, Joseph (Pope Benedict XVI). *Many Religions — One Covenant: Israel, the Church, and the World.* Translated by Graham Harrison. San Francisco: Ignatius Press, 1999.

———. *Truth and Tolerance: Christian Belief and World Religions.* Translated by Henry Taylor. San Francisco: Ignatius Press, 2004.

Swidler, Leonard J. *The Meaning of Life at the Edge of the Third Millennium.* Mahwah, N.J.: Paulist Press, 1992.

Whalen, William J. *Separated Brethren, Revised: A Review of Protestant, Anglican, Eastern Orthodox & Other Religions in the United States.* Huntington, Ind.: Our Sunday Visitor, 2002.

Made in the USA
Lexington, KY
28 August 2013